THE GAMEKEEPER'S BOY

THE GAMEKEEPER'S BOY

The story of a boy growing up on the
North Norfolk coast a century ago

by Mike Cringle
illustrated by Anne Cringle

The Larks Press

Published by the Larks Press
Ordnance Farmhouse, Guist Bottom, Dereham,
Norfolk NR20 5PF
01328 829207
Larks.Press@btinternet.com
Website: www.booksatlarkspress.co.uk

Printed by the Lanceni Press,
Garrood Drive, Fakenham, Norfolk

October 2001
Reprinted 2002, 2006

Reprinted 2009, 2013 by Newprint and Design Ltd
Garrood Drive, Fakenham, Norfolk

British Library Cataloguing-in-Publication Data
A catalogue record for this book is available
from the British Library

FRONT COVER
Watercolour of 'Cley 1896'
by M. Hurst

The map reproduced on pages 66 and 67 is based upon the 1958 Ordnance
Survey map with the permission of Her Majesty's Stationery Office
© Crown copyright MC 100014845

ISBN 978 1 904006 01 9

Foreword

My father, Pat Cringle, was born on the North Norfolk coast in 1891, and in his youth saw the end of a style of life that had hardly changed in generations, but which would soon be gone for ever. Much later in his long life, he looked back and wrote down many of the things that he remembered from those distant days, and so passed his story on for future generations. This book is based on his recollections of the shipwrecks and excitements, tragedies and comic events that made up his life as a boy and young man.

Chapter One

The sea and our family seem to have had a long and close relationship, and my father Patrick Cringle came of a long line of seafaring folk. The family name appears in old churchyards, which lie very close to the sea on the north Norfolk coast, and also in old trade directories which list master mariners and the like. This seagoing family came originally from the Isle of Man, and in the eighteenth century was no doubt engaged in the busy coastal trade that went on around the British Isles in those days. Barley from East Anglia to Ireland seems to have been an important cargo, and that was probably the reason they were here in the first place.

A hundred years later, in the mid-nineteenth century, there were several Cringles still here, and still sailing their boats round the coastal waters. One was the captain of the packet ship, *London Trader,* sailing regularly from Wapping up and down the east coast. Another was the famous Captain Cringle who, at about the same period, became well known for having seen, in the course of a voyage to Australia, a sea serpent in mid-Atlantic. It was a certain sighting, confirmed by his first officer and others aboard the ship, but he always said in later life that he bitterly regretted seeing the pesky thing. From the moment he reported it he was doomed never to be free of someone asking him about it, or just pulling his leg.

Judging by those tombstones in coastal churchyards, there must have been a fair number of the family still living on or near the Norfolk coast at that time, but later they seem to have thinned out, and by the beginning of the next century there are few of them still to be found. The coming of the railways and the decline in coastal shipping probably had a lot to do with it.

My grandfather, Tom Cringle, was a gamekeeper, and as far as I know never went further to sea than a wildfowler's punt would take him. His son Patrick, my father, though he spent his entire childhood and youth in Wells, and on the marshes and shore, and whose feet must have been permanently wet with salt water, never actually went to sea in a professional sense either. But the shipping, and the comings and goings of the harbour, and the gossip of the old sailors and fishermen, must have fascinated him. Stories of shipwrecks and heroic rescues imprinted themselves in his young mind, and as an old man he could still remember very clearly these stories, and events such as the building of the memorial on the quay to commemorate the *Eliza Adams* disaster.

This tragedy, and the loss of many lifeboat men, had happened years before he was born, but was still vivid in people's memories, and when a public meeting was called, much later on, to raise funds for the monument on the quay, young Pat, full of interest and curiosity, was there.

It was an event charged with emotion, even then, long after the men had died, and while the chairman was opening the meeting from the platform, several old men in the hall took over and began to sing, 'Pull for the shore, sailor, pull for the shore!' Soon everyone was joining in, and the people on the platform had to wait with a good grace for the singing to die down before they could make themselves heard again. At last Tom Kew, one of the only two men to survive, was able to speak; then the money was soon raised, and the memorial built.

The actual story of the loss of most of the crew of the lifeboat *Eliza Adams* is brief and simple. The boat was in service at Wells from about 1870, and she was a good lifeboat of the type usual in her day, propelled by sail and oars, and self-righting.

On the wild October day when these events took place there had already been no less than three wrecks, driven on to the sands between Wells and Holkham by a savage northerly gale. The crews of two of them, small shallow draught boats, had managed to get ashore, hauled through the breakers by fishermen with ropes. But the lifeboat had to fight her way out in the teeth of the gale during the afternoon to rescue the crew of a bigger ship, the *Shanon Rose* from Whitby.

When she was safely back at the quay again, and putting the seven men from the *Shanon Rose* ashore, the coxswain of the lifeboat remarked that the seas were the worst he had ever known, but that the *Eliza Adams* had behaved perfectly. Even so, the lifeboat men were still soaked to the skin and exhausted; then another distress rocket was seen, to the east of the harbour, and they had to make ready for sea again.

Four of the crew were too tired to carry on, but volunteers from the fishermen on the quay immediately took their places, and the lifeboat was off again, down the harbour channel towards the thundering white breakers that marked the edge of the open sea.

It was a long hard row against the gale, and even with the new men every effort had to be made to keep reserves of energy for what was bound to be a difficult rescue when the stricken ship was

reached. At times like this the steam tug *Promise* was brought into use, for although she could only be used in the relatively calm waters inside the harbour, she would give the tired men some respite as the lifeboat was given a tow as far as the open water. Once there, they dropped the tow-rope and bent to their oars again amidst the rolling breakers and blowing spume.

By this time the ship that was in distress, called the *Ocean Queen*, was aground a mile to the east of the harbour entrance, so the lifeboat headed out to sea to get beyond the worst of the broken water, and then set sail to run down to the wreck on a broad reach. The use of sail, even in these horrific conditions, was normal practice, and gave exhausted oarsmen a chance to rest aching arms. Watchers on the shore could see all this happening quite clearly, though some of the time only the peak of the lifeboat's sail was visible as they plunged into a trough between heaving swells.

Then, just as the *Eliza Adams* could be seen approaching the *Ocean Queen*, now covered in breaking waves as her crew took refuge in the rigging, the lifeboat disappeared between breakers yet again, and failed to reappear. There were long drawn-out seconds as the watchers on the shore waited for a glimpse of the sail, but it was not to be seen.

At last the hull of the lifeboat did appear again, but upside down, and to the horror of the onlookers, she was not righting herself. Men began to run along the beach towards where they reckoned that the disabled lifeboat would be blown ashore, but then they saw that she had not moved from where she had capsized. The inverted hull seemed to be anchored. One lifeboat man was seen drifting in his cork jacket amongst the breakers, and he was eagerly hauled ashore, but he was the only one. That man was Tom Kew, and when he had recovered himself he described what had happened.

As they had neared the *Ocean Queen*, in very shallow water, a single wave, twice as high as any other, bore down on them; and even as the coxswain brought the lifeboat's head up to it, they were rolled over, and the mast must have stuck in the sand. Then the anchor came loose and fell out of her, and there she was trapped and pounded by the same seas as the ship they were trying to save. Those who could, tried to hold on to the inverted hull, but soon became exhausted; then the mast broke and the boat righted herself, but only one man, thrown back by the sea, was inside. He and Tom Kew got to the shore, but all the others died.

Ironically, the crew of the *Ocean Queen,* though terrified, had never been in mortal danger. Their ship did not break up in the storm and, as the tide ebbed, they were all able to walk ashore.

—⊰⟡⊱—

The whole of the north Norfolk coast is strewn with the wrecks of ships. The geography of the area makes it almost inevitable because it forms a large bay with the Lincolnshire coast, the other side of the Wash, and in the days of sail a north-easterly wind was always likely to trap ships in it. Any skipper worth his salt was well aware of that, and they all took great care to avoid that particular trap; but it took a very clever man to forecast a north-easterly gale more than a few hours ahead, and then there was always sheer bad luck to contend with.

In its way it was as dangerous, with the wind in the wrong direction, as the more famous, or infamous, Bay of Biscay. But the prevailing winds are from the west, so most of the time it was a perfectly safe sailing ground if you avoided the sand banks. Many of course did this with great skill; but a few did not, for one reason or another, and even today the bones of old sailing ships can still be seen sticking up from the sands off Wells when the tide is well out. Pat knew them all by name, and their histories.

Such stories of the sea were all part of Pat's young life, and even such a well-remembered disaster had no real effect on his attitude to the wilderness of sea and shore and marshes that were his world; they probably represented adventure more than tragedy in his young mind. A shipwreck was also exciting.

One that he himself saw happened just to the west of Wells, beyond Holkham, off Overy Harbour.

A small type of coastal trader, locally called a 'billy-boy', had arrived from the north at dawn one morning carrying coal for Brancaster. She was called the *Brilliant,* and she anchored off Wells in a strong westerly wind, to wait for a fair tide and perhaps a more favourable slant in the wind to carry her along the coast to her destination.

Unluckily for her, as the wind did shift to the north it also began to increase and was soon a full gale. She remained in sight off Wells all day, and by that evening she was still in sight, just a mile or two further west off Holkham, but close-in and too near the shore for comfort. Up to then, no distress signal had been seen, but everyone knew that they were looking at a ship in a very dangerous position, and the lifeboat crew were warned to be ready.

As darkness closed in, the weather got even worse, and at about nine o'clock the expected rocket was at last seen. The lifeboat was launched, but by then the tide was rushing in with the full force of the gale behind it, and the men at the oars had to struggle for nearly an hour just to get clear of the broken water around the harbour mouth and reach the open sea.

Pat and a friend of his followed them down as far as they could on foot, and then watched them go, heaving at their oars in the northerly gale. Then the two boys set out at a run along the sandhills and the shore, past Holkham Gap, towards Overy Hill, where they reckoned the *Brilliant* was doomed to blow ashore.

It was night by now, but there was a moon showing fitfully through the scudding clouds, and when the boys reached the sandhills off Overy they could clearly see the stricken ship. She was frighteningly near the beach, only just outside a line of huge waves breaking on the shore. Her bows were pointed straight out to sea, obviously held by a dragging anchor, and it was clear that she must soon dig her keel into the hard sand and founder. As the boys, bent double against the wind, ran down the shore towards her they

knew that she was finished; a matter of minutes would see the waves foaming over her hull and beginning to break her up. Then the lifeboat appeared from seaward, driving through the breakers, and apparently trying to get into the lee of the *Brilliant*, the bowman of the lifeboat standing with a grapnel in his hand, looking for his chance to get a line into her rigging.

A few other people with a lantern had arrived at the scene by now, and they all stood and watched grimly, unable to lift a finger to help in the drama that was taking place within yards of them. Suddenly, as the lifeboat men were struggling to get into a position where they could take men off the stricken ship, a wave seemed to catch the lifeboat and lift it high in the air. Then, in an instant, with the men still rowing hard, the boat was driven up the beach, and left there.

The men were still bent at their oars, momentarily not comprehending what had happened to them, as the wave receded with much sucking of sand and shingle; the people on the shore gazed, stunned, at this incredible scene. Then the very next wave, surging over the *Brilliant,* brought the mizzen mast down; after that the main mast soon followed, and that was the end of her. With the lifeboat helpless on the beach the crew of the *Brilliant* were beyond reach, until at last each man was torn from the wreck by the storm, and washed up on to the dark shore.

Pat and his friend crept home in the early hours, awed by the sheer drama of what they had seen, slept for a few hours, and then in the morning trudged back along the sand dunes to Overy beach, compelled somehow to go and look upon the scene again. But in the cold daylight all was changed; the great tragic tableau of the previous night was over, and only two or three local men stood on the shore amongst scattered wreckage, talking it over in subdued voices.

—⚜—

Chapter Two

To the crew of a ship approaching Wells in those days, up the channel from the open sea, the town would have appeared, from a distance, much as it does now: the marshes to the east and the sea bank to the west, the grey stone of the quay, and the jumble of buildings rising steeply beyond it up Staithe Street. But on closer inspection old Wells was quite a different place from the modern holiday resort.

The quay itself was a more open space than it is now, with no walls, and railway sidings where trucks for loading or unloading ships were constantly shunted about. Most of the buildings facing on to the waterfront were workaday stores or maltings, with a sprinkling of cottages and pubs between them. The people there were sailors and fishermen working on their boats, or old retired men of the sea who liked to stand about and pass the time of day with each other, and see that things were being done properly. The quay had always been the centre of social and business life for them, and they would always gravitate towards it, even with nothing much to do there but gossip with old friends, or drink a slow pint of twopenny ale at one of the pubs.

Apart from a good collection of shops in one or two streets, most of the buildings were very much connected with the sea, from the modest cottages of fishermen that lined the many yards, to a few handsome houses belonging to sea captains, and mansions occupied by well-to-do merchants and their families.

There were buildings that have disappeared from the life of the town altogether now: smoke houses, where in season vast amounts of herring became kippers and bloaters, stabling for all the many horses used about the little port, and blacksmiths' forges where their iron shoes were made and fitted. There were slaughter houses for all the meat eaten in the town, or taken for ships' stores and of course many businesses, small and large, which existed because ships have to be built, and repaired, and kept in good order, and properly supplied with whatever they need.

Pat's father, being a keeper, lived in an estate lodge, but it was a lodge that overlooked the marshes rather than the parkland of the big estate. The family might no longer make their living from the sea, but they still saw it every day of their lives; and the view from their home was straight over the saltings to that line of blue or grey that always marked the horizon beyond the distant sand-hills. Young Pat must have looked at it each morning when he got up, and noticed without even thinking about it whether the sea was in a benign or angry mood.

Like everyone who lives near the sea, he soon became aware of its danger, and the care with which wise people treat it; but to a young lad it was often also a good friend, providing opportunities for making a few shillings in times when money was a pretty rare item in a boy's pocket. Sometimes, especially after a northerly gale, things like empty kegs or good timber could be garnered from the beach and sold. Fish were also saleable, at any rate for a few pence. Pat was always ready to make the best of what fate offered; one of the first jobs that came his way, was when someone up at the big estate decided that a warden was needed for the tern colony on the beach. This gave him the chance, at least for a time, of earning an actual wage for doing what he liked best,

In those days bird sanctuaries and nature reserves had scarcely been thought of, but there was a well-known ternary on a part of the beach at Wells, and someone had decided that it would be a good idea to keep an eye on the breeding terns there. The word was passed down from the estate office that young Pat could have the job; and his father told him that he could have the use of a houseboat that was moored in a creek, not far away from the stretch of sand and shingle where the birds nested.

The pay would not be very much, but Pat could live there on the houseboat for a month or two, and be captain of his own ship and master of all he surveyed. He could hardly wait to get a few things together, and get out there.

The great salt marsh that stretches along the coast from Wells to Blakeney somehow remains, even to the present day, miraculously wild and lonely. Even in summer, when the cars are nose to tail along the coast road, and Wells itself is so full of visitors that you would not be surprised to see them falling over the edge of the quay, the marshes are blessedly empty of human kind. Leave the crowds on the beach and in Staithe Street, wade over a creek or two, and you are soon alone; even the noise of them is left behind.

There is a place on the seaward side of the marsh, only a mile or two from the town, that is as quiet as anywhere you will find in England. A broad, sandy creek, with only a trickle of water in it at low tide, suddenly widens into a deep, dark pool. Not like the usual shallow pools where fish might be caught, but dark and mysterious, not inches but several feet deep. The tall grass and scrubby bushes that grow here and there on the marsh overshadow it on one side, and the water always looks cold and uninviting. You hardly ever seem to see anybody there; even the few people who make their way over to the sand-hills in the summer seldom go near that particular place.

From there, on the edge of the empty sands that stretch all the way to Blakeney Point, the holiday crowds are completely out of sight. Wells town is just a cluster of tiny houses in the distance, far over the hazy marsh, at the foot of the low, inland hills. Few sounds from the outside world seem to reach there. A very peaceful place, but with that vague uneasiness that lonely places often seem to have. If the occasional family picnic party does find its way there, they seldom stay long.

Once, long ago, a bank was built along the side of the marsh there, across the course of that creek, to deflect the flow and ebb of the tides. It is a trick that has often been used to increase the scour of the tidal flow through the harbour and keep it free of silting sands. But the sea, which does not like being redirected by man, broke through again with the help of a big tide and a northerly gale. The new bank was breached, and the channel returned to its old course, the sea pouring through with such force that a great hole was dug out, deep into the mud where the bank had been. It is the remains of this pit, even silted up as it is after all these years, that forms the deep pool. It was called Tebble's Hole by local people, and Pat would never forget how it had got that name.

The bank had been broken, and the hole dug out by the incoming tide just a few years before he was given the job of looking after the ternery, and it was still deep and wide with steep, muddy sides. Young Pat knew it well, as he knew all the rest of the marsh.

He was very pleased with his job, and spent a lot of time on the houseboat, living what might seem a very solitary life for a young man, with only the wildfowl for company; sometimes he hardly spoke to another person from dawn to dusk. Thus it happened that when one day there was a hue and cry after someone who had disappeared, he knew nothing about it until late that afternoon.

A man called Tebble had set out from Wells, walking over the marsh in the general direction of the shore to the east of the town, and had not been seen since. The danger of a drowning is always present in the minds of people who live near the marsh, and the alarm had been raised. Search parties went out, and eventually Pat met up with one of them.

When he heard the news he remembered something he had noticed earlier in the day as he passed by the deep pool, and as the search party went on their way he went back to the pool, to have another look. Sure enough, there were scrapes and marks on the side that suggested that something heavy had slithered down into the dark water; but by now the spring evening was closing in, it was becoming chilly, would soon be dark, and the other searchers had vanished. Suddenly it was very lonely on the edge of the shore, and the young warden felt disinclined to spend the night alone in the old houseboat. He followed the search parties back to the town and spent that night at home with his parents.

In the morning he led some of the men back to the pool again and they took lengths of cod-line and hooks to drag through it. It was a difficult job, and it took a long time to search the deepest parts, but at last the hooks caught into something deep down.

After several false starts, it was hauled laboriously to the surface and lay there on the mud like a sodden bundle of old clothes, while water cascaded from it back down the steep bank. The body of poor Tebble had been found, and Tebble's Hole had acquired its name.

⋇⋇⟡⋇⋇

Chapter Three

My father, as a young boy in Wells, does not seem to have spent much of his time in the serious pursuit of learning. He had to go to school, without doubt, and he certainly learned to write good English at some time, a tribute to his long-suffering schoolmaster; for later in life he left endless bits of diary and notes about those early days. But his recorded memories of those years are all of the many and varied activities of him and his friends outside school hours; sometimes of the more serious side of daily life, but also of the many ways they used to entertain themselves. Most of the things that are so important to the young these days did not even exist; but even then, at the very beginning of the twentieth century, he was able to record an early example of football fever, and even soccer hooliganism.

Before that time football had not figured very prominently locally; in fact organized matches seem to have only recently started when he was a boy. Cricket had been even more foreign to the local lads, and when played at all was a highly informal event, with a seven-pound corned beef tin used as a wicket. The chief sporting interests seems to have been kite-flying on the sea wall, and, rather surprisingly, marbles played on the quay.

Marbles was a very serious game, and not by any means just for the young. Typical teams, in those days, were made up of two or three retired sea captains, maltsters, several long-whiskered old fishermen, and possibly the harbour master. The marbles used for these tournaments were of two types: light ones, roughly the same as children might use today, and another more serious type of marble called the 'iron toy'. This latter was a more formidable instrument altogether, being a small iron ball weighing about three ounces, specially cast for serious players at the local iron foundry. Some people disapproved of the heavy iron marble, and so two distinct schools existed side by side.

In the first, that used ordinary marbles or the glass stoppers from ginger beer bottles, an elegant style was used in which the marble was balanced on the index finger, and then flicked neatly forward with a twitch of the thumb. The iron toy men, on the other hand, merely hurled theirs with as much force as possible, relying on weight and brute force to beat the opposition.

It was the older men who played in these serious games, and also in the dominoes and draughts tournaments that took place at the wooden benches and tables near the old lifeboat house. The young men and boys seldom took part. Before the coming of the town football team their sporting events were casual contests such as a swimming race in the harbour, or a foot race down the bank to the beach and back, a course of two miles.

Another highly informal sport was provided by a retired showman who lived at Wells. His name was Broady, and he ran a coconut shy that must have been a relic of his days on the road. Every Saturday night when the weather was fine Broady could be seen with his pony cart, packed with his gear, trundling along to his favourite pitch close by three pubs. There he used to set up his canvas screens and his long spiked iron cups for the coconuts, and wait for business.

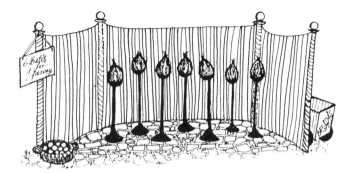

Nothing much usually happened until the nearby pubs began to disgorge their customers at closing time, but then business became brisk as young men set out to prove their superiority by seeing who could do best with wooden ball against coconut.

Broady's ex-fairground entertainment was well known and popular for years, and was the accepted way of disposing of any odd pence left over when the pubs closed on Saturday nights.

But to return to the football scene, which was just becoming important in the town. A team had been formed; there were fixtures against surrounding villages, and people were suddenly beginning to discover the great pleasure of thrashing the opposition.

The match became the event of the week, and attendance at the town football ground, a meadow on the beach road, was becoming quite good. No one had thought of charging an entrance fee, and anybody who had nothing else to do was likely to turn up. Even some of the old men left their dominoes and draughts on the quay and sauntered down to cheer the home team. No one ever cheered the opposing team, and if they scored a goal the event was always greeted with a dead silence, possibly broken by the mocking screech of a passing seagull.

It had been a tense game in which there had been plenty of hard-fought action but no one had managed to score; and in the final moments of the match all those on the field, players and watchers, were already assuming that it would end in a dull but safe draw, with the home team's honour intact. Then one of the Ryburgh men suddenly sneaked the ball in between the Wells goal posts. The town supporters and players assumed, to a man, that it had been offside; and watched with horror as the referee allowed it.

Then the final whistle went, and Wells was down, one goal to nil. Incredulous, the home supporters booed Ryburgh off the pitch, and out of the field, and pursued them all the way through the town to the railway station. Odd apple cores, left-over refreshments, or anything else that came to hand were thrown, and the visiting team ended up huddled together on the platform, waiting pathetically for their train to arrive, surrounded by a more or less juvenile, but still seriously hostile, crowd chanting, 'Rotten Ryburgh, rotten Ryburgh!' Only the simultaneous arrival of the train and the local policeman cooled the situation, and the crowd, as they say, melted away.

This policeman seems to have figured large in the lives of the Wells boys in those days, and the guardian of the law they knew was a very different creature from a modern police officer, hung round with hi-tech equipment, and usually inside a police car. The blue clad figure, which was only too familiar to them, carried but one piece of equipment, a swagger cane, used for swiping at boys and in frequent use. It was he who might be waiting at the bottom of a garden wall when boys scrambled over it with a load of someone else's apples, or who spoilt the fun in winter when they innocently constructed a slide down one of the steep Wells streets.

Young Pat and his friends knew perfectly well that the policeman was usually going to win; that was what he was supposed to do, but it did not stop them tormenting him when they got the chance.

That chance often came in the winter, when night came early. The town streets were only illuminated by a feeble gaslight here and there, and yards and alleys were pitch dark. This gave the boys a natural advantage, and they loved it. Their repertoire of annoying tricks against adults and authority included the usual ones like activating door-knockers with long lengths of string, but local geography gave them one favourite and unusual game.

This centred on the railway sidings along the water front, used in loading and unloading ships at the quay, where there were often empty wagons left at night. Shunting these wagons about was the game that some of the bigger boys liked to play, and on many an occasion the policeman had to leave his tea and go down to the harbour to do something about the noise. The enjoyable rumble and crash of the wagons colliding on the dark quay, the shouts and laughter of the boys, and the clatter of their boots as they quickly disappeared into those unlit alleys and yards brought few smiles to his lips.

Things came to a head one day when several wagons, carefully placed to unload a ship first thing in the morning, were found to be dispersed all over the length of the sidings. It caused much waste of time for a shipmaster keen to sail on the tide; official complaints followed. The next night the forces of law and order decided that they'd had enough, and laid an ambush.

When the boys arrived, ready for another evening's entertainment, they did not know that their enemy was already there, hiding in an empty wagon and waiting for them. As they put their shoulders against it and it began to move, the policeman hurled himself out of it, cane swinging, and managed to land several shrewd blows. The lads thought that this was a particularly mean trick.

The ultimate brush with the law happened on one Guy Fawkes' night, and ended not in the usual swish of the swagger cane, but an actual court appearance for some of the boys.

The fifth of November used to be a big occasion. A fair was held on the Buttlands with stalls and side shows. Special rock was on sale and the ever popular coconut shy was set up. Everyone gathered to enjoy the fun and, as darkness drew on, a bonfire was lit. Then things began to get exciting. Fireworks exploded, flames roared up into the sky, sparks flew everywhere, and the evening ended with what they called the tar-barrel run.

For this, old barrels well soaked in tar were brought from the town gasworks, and were pushed into the remains of the fire as it died down. Then, when they were blazing away fiercely, a gang of older youths would fish them out of the fire with long poles, and trundle them, belching flame, round and round the Buttlands.

This strange, wild scene may well have had its origin long before Guy Fawkes and gunpowder plots. Perhaps it was a memory of some old Viking fire ritual that used to be enacted when many-oared longboats lay in Norfolk creeks.

Whatever the long-forgotten origin of the custom may have been, it was still being carried on with enthusiasm when Pat was a boy, and he and his friends were watching on that particular night as the fire-spouting barrels were being prodded round by their excited attendants. Round and round the dying fire they went, faster and faster; and then suddenly one shot off out of the circle towards a dark corner, where a familiar figure in blue uniform lurked, quietly watching. Lurid flames picked out an answering twinkle from polished buttons, and then the dark figure leaped out of his corner, just missing the fiery tar-barrel but losing his helmet as he leapt. It disappeared in the blazing tar. The boys who had allowed their barrel to wander disappeared very promptly too, into the darkness beyond the firelight, but not before faces had been noticed, and names scribbled down in the official notebook.

The nearest magistrate's court was at Walsingham, and that was where two of the boys, with great trepidation, had to appear. The exhilaration of the night had long left them and they were filled with apprehension about being accused of trying to set fire to a policeman, and what might happen to them. They had heard about the grim Victorian cells in the old prison, just a matter of yards from the courthouse. But the magistrate must have had a soft spot for youth, or a strong sense of humour, or perhaps he did not much like the policeman either. He listened to the story, found the boys guilty of unruly behaviour, fined them sixpence, and sent them home.

Chapter Four

A magistrate's court was probably dealing with a light load of crime in such a place, at such a time. Poachers, bicycles without proper lights, no doubt the odd petty crime, but most people, if poor, still seem to have been very law-abiding, except possibly for a little light smuggling.

All seaside places have their smuggling traditions, and Wells is no exception. In the days when the harbour was a-bustle with ships loading and unloading, and schooners and billy-boys were often lying three deep against the quay, the illegal movement of a good deal of wine and spirits must have gone on. Several buildings along the waterfront were reputed to have had secret cellars, often filled with barrels and kegs that had never been seen by a revenue man; but the centre of this cottage industry was said to be the old Royal Standard. This fine old building, now called Standard House, still stands at the east end of the main quay, and in those days was the staging inn from which coaches left for Norwich and King's Lynn. It was in a perfect position for the trade, and became so notorious that the local boys called the landlord the king of the smugglers.

Many a beady eye must have watched his activities closely, but he seems to have got away with moving on illegal goods on a regular basis. One of the tricks, which even the boys knew about, was to time the departure of a load to when the customs man was at the pool, where an incoming ship might lie, a mile down the harbour channel towards the sea. It was said that several pony traps were often seen coming and going at about the same time, as a few kegs were distributed to other local hostelries.

Pat was never involved in any of this, even if he had wanted to; a gamekeeper's son was not likely to be trusted by someone involved in that trade. But he used to like to go and hang about round the old pub and watch the goings on of the sailors and fishermen, and listen to their tales and the singing. The Standard, apart from its smuggling reputation, was well known also for the quality of the singing and dancing that went on there, and such things were important then. There was a strong tradition in Norfolk in those days for step dancing in particular, and the boys, who were too young to be allowed in, often used to watch through the windows; many years later Pat could still quote the words and sing snatches of popular shanties.

Music and dancing seem to have been just as important as the flowing ale to the men who frequented that house, and there was a certain ritual that started it off every evening. First the fiddler would arrive, with his violin wrapped in a cloth, and he would quietly take his seat in a corner. Soon someone would buy him a pint of beer, the only payment he ever received, and he would still just sit there, and chat perhaps, but with one eye on any of those round about whom he knew to be a good dancer.

Then, when he felt the moment was right, he would casually unwrap his fiddle and draw the bow across its strings, and one of the seamen, who no doubt had been waiting for the signal, would put down his drink and amidst shouts of encouragement move into the centre of the floor. The fiddle player would strike up a hornpipe, and amidst much shuffling and stamping the evening's entertainment was under way. And it would go on, step dancing and singing of old sea songs alternating, until closing time.

Young Pat listened and watched, and never forgot these scenes, and the old songs and stories that were repeated again and again.

THE BOLD PRINCESS ROYAL
a favourite sea song

'Twas the fourteenth of February when we sailed from the land
On the bold Princess Royal bound for Newfoundland.
With fourteen bright seamen for the ship's company,
To the eastward and southward then westward sailed we.

We scarce had been sailing for two days or three
When the man at our masthead strange sails he did see
They bore down upon us to see what we were
And under his mizzen peak strange colours he wore.

He drove down towards us and hove alongside,
With a big speaking trumpet "where ye bound for?" he cried.
Our captain being aft my boys, he answered just so,
"We are from fair London, bound down to Bilbo".

"Then shake out your reefs, my boys, and heave your ship to,
For I have a long letter to send there by you".
"Yes, we'll shake out our reefs, my boys, and we'll heave our
ship to,
But in Bilbo harbour, not alongside of you!"

Then he chased us to windward all that live long day,
He chased us to windward, but he made no headway.
He fired shots after us, but could not prevail,
For the bold *Princess Royal* soon showed them her tail.

When out in the Atlantic, and out of their grasp,
Our captain came forward with a bottle and a glass.
Go you down to your grog my boys, and drink with good cheer,
On the bold *Princess Royal* you have nothing to fear.

Needless to say, many of these stories were of shipwreck and rescues, but many were also of lighter incidents that amused and diverted the town from time to time, and of the odd characters involved in them.

One tale that made everyone chuckle for years afterwards was about a man called Lump, a name that, like most of those amongst sailors and fishermen, was probably not given him at his christening. He seems to have come to Wells as a result of being saved from one of the many wrecks, and made it clear that he had no intention of ever going to sea again. He made a living of sorts doing odd jobs along the quay, loading and unloading ships, or any other casual work that came his way. When he had any money he was known for getting rid of it again as quickly as possible in one of the many waterside pubs.

One of the jobs he helped with was manning the local fire engine, a machine that had to be dragged and manoeuvred by hand, in and out of the narrow alleys and yards, whenever there was an emergency. On the day he became famous the alarm had been raised for a fire at a linen draper's shop, and he was there doing his bit of dragging and pumping. The fire had started amongst the bales of cloth in the store at the back, and thick smoke was billowing out of the front of the shop, but it was not too serious a conflagration, and was soon damped down. But although the fire was out, it took a long time to clear up afterwards, and it was not until late in the evening, when the fire engine was due to be hauled back to its shed, that it was noticed that Lump was missing.

Consternation reigned. Was there a singed body lying under still-smoking bales of cloth somewhere? Then someone remembered seeing Lump climbing up a ladder and going through an upstairs window. The upper storey was relatively undamaged, so the ladder was set up again, and others went in the same way, to find the missing fireman sound asleep, and snoring peacefully. The room contained a large and obviously comfortable bed, and a large but empty whiskey bottle. It was generally understood that on entering the bedroom Lump had seen the then full bottle of whiskey, realized its potential danger in a burning building, and had bravely dealt with the problem by drinking it.

The only difficulty was getting Lump out of the room again, he being in no state to see the ladder, much less descend it. However, men of the sea knew how to deal with this sort of problem, and a hoist was soon attached to a beam, a rope made fast round Lump, and he was pushed out of the window and lowered to mother earth. The fire pump returned to base with him holding on to it rather than pushing or pulling, and all was well. But of course no one ever forgot the story of Lump the fireman.

Another resident who had to stand years of leg-pulling on account of one foolish act was a retired businessman, from inland somewhere, who came to live in Wells, and decided that he would like to have a boat like everyone else.

He got together a good supply of timber and all the other necessities, and set to building one in the front room of his house. He worked away at it for months, made a splendid job of it, beautifully varnished and painted, and then discovered, to everyone's huge enjoyment, that it was too big to go out through the door.

With much help from grinning neighbours, first the door, and then the door frame, was removed. Still the shiny new boat could not be extracted until a few bricks were knocked out too, and then at last it was dragged out through the jagged hole in the wall.

The whole event had taken on a sort of festival mood by now, with a rapidly growing crowd, and many hands took hold of the boat and lifted it up into the air; he was lifted up too and placed in it. Then he and his boat were carried with much horseplay through the streets, and launched into the harbour.

Local characters were discussed endlessly. There was the butcher with the donkey and cart who always visited the same pubs, in the same order, every time he went out. One day he got his donkey cart ready, and was then called away. Hours later, the donkey and cart was found standing outside the pub that was always the last one on his calling schedule. The town laughed about this one for years, because the donkey had been observed going from one pub to the next all the morning, and waiting outside each one for half an hour, exactly as though he was being driven by his owner.

Then there was Hector, who made a habit of dancing with the performing bears that still came round in those days; he also used to make friends with organ-grinders' monkeys and was famous for conducting the German bands that visited from time to time. What the German bands, the monkeys and the dancing bears thought about Hector is not recorded.

There was also the old fisherman who owned an equally old and rickety, four-bore, muzzle-loading goose gun, who was remembered for just one witty reply to a visitor's question about why he used such a crazy old bit of ironmongery to shoot with. The gun was well-known, apart from its enormous size, for the great gout of flame that shot out whenever he pulled the trigger, and he told the visiting expert, 'Well, that do give me two chances. If the shot go in front and miss, that old goose may still fly into the flame and come down cooked.'

A popular character whom Pat knew well, called Frank Hook, was fated to become the central figure in a local mystery that was never solved, and by chance the young boy was the only witness of what happened. Frank was one of the old men who were often to be seen chatting over a glass of beer at one of the pubs, or on a fine summer's day sitting on a bench watching the shipping in the harbour. He had a long grey beard, and wore the white sweater and peaked cap of a retired sailor; he had tales to tell of all the oceans of the world. He had spent his life in blue-water ships, and now, as an old man, had come back to the shallow waters of the North Norfolk coast, where he made a living of sorts fishing for shrimps in Holkham Bay.

He was a great singer of the old sailors' songs too, and was a favourite performer at the Shipwright's Arms on a Saturday night. He must have felt that he had just about finished with the sea after spending most of his life upon it, but the sea had not finished with him.

There are many tales of dire wrecks and tragedies caused by the fierce northerly gales that can tear at this coast from time to time, but the warm south wind can be a force to contend with too. When the wind is in that quarter the air on the quay may hardly seem to move at all, but a short way off-shore, away from the sheltering land, the fitful zephyr can become a stiff breeze. Small boats heel suddenly as their crews lean out, and even a well-handled yacht can have difficulties beating in against a wind that gusts and drops and shifts, partly blanketed by the sand dunes. Old Frank Hook must have had plenty of experience of every wind that blows, but it was this warm, friendly, but treacherous breeze that finally got him.

Between Holkham and Wells, when the tide is out, there is a

stretch of water that can be seen to the west of the harbour channel, running towards it from Holkham Bay. It looks as if it might be an entrance to the harbour, but is separated from it by a spit of sand. This false channel, forming an elongated lagoon at low water, is called the West Lake, and small craft approaching Wells can wait in it for the tide to rise high enough for them to get up the real harbour channel. It was here that Pat, walking home along the shore from the Holkham direction one evening, happened to notice the old man and his shrimp-boat.

The old sailor had been out as usual, fishing in the bay, and was sailing home as the tide flowed. Coming from that direction it was natural for an experienced man with a shallow-draught boat to take a short cut up the West Lake, and then cross over the sand bar into the main channel as the tide rose. Casually Pat noticed him sail close-hauled up the West Lake, well reefed down against the brisk southerly breeze, then luff up, drop his sail, and anchor. It was the normal thing to do while he waited for the tide to rise, and so the young boy was only seeing, as he walked along, the ordinary scene of a lone fisherman coming home on the evening tide. The light was fading, and he went on his way, hurrying home, to be scolded for being late as usual. He had no idea of the fisherman he had seen being in any danger, and had forgotten all about what he had seen by the time he went to bed.

The following morning, the first thing he heard was that Frank Hook had not been seen that night; his boat had not come up to the quay with the tide, and no one knew where he was. Had he left his boat at the pool, a mile below the town? Had it gone further on up the creek somewhere? Perhaps he had just gone to sleep in it somewhere, and would shortly reappear. But Frank Hook was never seen again.

Weeks later an anchor was found buried in the sand. It was roughly where Pat had seen him, and it might have been his. So his anchor rope might have parted while he waited for the tide; but after that? No one ever knew. But whatever went wrong, as he waited out there in shallow water just a mile from home, the twilight deepening into darkness, it seems certain his boat did not sink. If it had, some sign of it or its contents would surely have come to light sooner or later. Apart from the anchor, if it *was* his anchor, nothing was ever seen.

The old sailor, and his boat and all, must surely have been carried away out to sea by the treacherous southerly breeze. Frank Hook simply went back to the salt water where he had spent most of his life, and disappeared for ever.

Chapter Five

For young Pat, as the son of a gamekeeper on one of the great English estates in the very early years of this century, life had a quality that has disappeared now. He was living in a world that, within its own strict boundaries, was secure and oddly carefree. Such people were not well off by present-day standards, but they held a position in that little world that was unchallenged, and the future seemed to hold few hazards. A good gamekeeper held a respected place, and it would be assumed that he would live out his working life there, retire eventually to a little cottage somewhere on that same estate, and die there. And his son would very likely follow in his footsteps.

But for Pat that was not quite how he saw his own future. As a teenager he was already working with his father of course; he had done his job as a temporary bird warden, and might have been slipping into that comfortable routine that would eventually see him following a similar career. But Pat had noticed a snag – most of the time he was not being paid any real money.

Young boys helped their fathers as a matter of course, lived at home, and only got such pocket money or tips as might come their way by good fortune. 'What else do you need?' said his father, Tom. 'You live at home, your mother feeds you free. If you went somewhere else you might earn a few bob, but all your wages would go in board and lodging. You're better off at home.' But this young lad wanted to earn some money for himself. He wanted to be able to buy things. He wanted a gun and a pair of field-glasses like his father. More than that, he probably wanted to feel the independence of having a few gold sovereigns of his own. He knew perfectly well that there was little to be gained by leaving his home and going for a job on one of the surrounding farms. Being young and strong he could easily enough have done that and earned a few shillings a week for himself; but as his father said, he would have been no better off. Still, Pat felt, there must be opportunities to make a little money, if you kept your eyes open and watched for what chance might bring.

The very first chance came by way of his father, who may well have thought a little taste of working with someone else might be a good idea. Another keeper who worked on the same estate un-expectedly lost his assistant, just as he was in the middle of the important seasonal occupation of culling the jack hares. This is an almost impossible job for a man by himself, but there was no one else available, and Patrick suddenly found himself being offered a job at four and sixpence a week, and his food. Tom said he could spare him for a week or two, and off he went.

The culling of hares was a strange job, though probably not for young Patrick, who had grown up in this particular world. It hardly sounds like a serious job of work, for the keeper and his assistant to saunter apparently aimlessly round the estate, until they came upon a place of great hare activity. This would usually be an open grassy area, busy with jack hares prancing about and showing off to the females. There had to be a suitable large tree close by.

Now, hares are not stupid, and if a man happened to saunter too close to them, however casually, they would inevitably move away and continue their courting exercises somewhere else; but this wily old gamekeeper had a plan. He and his young assistant would walk casually towards the tree, and then he would stop there, out of sight, and the boy would walk on. It was assumed, and correctly it seems, that the jack hares, with their minds on the does, would not have noticed that two men approached the tree and only one left it. So when the boy appeared again, and began very gently to drive them towards that tree, there was a fair chance that one or two would go near enough to it to be within shot. That was the theory, and Patrick was soon good enough to produce frequent success for the keeper with his gun, even, by deft driving, to make a left and a right shot possible.

Thus Patrick got on well with his first employer, and the sun shone on his first job for a time. But then hare-culling became less urgent, and he found himself expected to do less amusing and congenial jobs, such as cleaning out the ferret hutches and taking the dogs out for exercise, even, at last, being given a spade and told to make himself useful in the garden. Patrick did not know, or perhaps did not want to know, how to be useful with a garden spade, and that job petered out. But he had struck out for himself, away from home, and had made a few shillings; and he was ready for whatever the world had to offer him next, which, as it happened, was a bit of serious fishing.

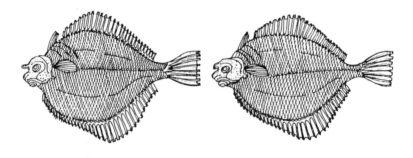

He had a friend called Young Ben by everyone along the sea front at Wells. His father, of course, was Old Ben, a fisherman of great experience who would occasionally pass on some of his knowledge to his son and young Pat. Old Ben had been a real professional deep-sea fisherman, and had spent most of his life working on the fishing boats out of Yarmouth or Hull; such was his wide, almost scientific, interest in the ways of fish that he had much useful advice to pass on.

Even when he was not at sea but at home in Wells, he still spent his time fishing, no doubt to the exasperation of his wife. But when he was approached by Young Ben and Patrick, who intimated that they were ready to try to make some real money, and didn't mind how hard they had to work, he took them under his wing. 'Nobody can make much out of the fishing these days,' he said, 'but I can tell you how to catch some big 'uns, and make a few bob. There's good fish if you know where to look for them, but most of the boys about here don't know what they're doing.'

He had studied what went on under the surface of the sea for many years, and knew that fish move about all the time, according to the weather and the time of day or night. Most of the local boys, if they heard that someone had a good catch, would all go along to the same place as soon as they could, to get some of the same fish, not realising that by then the fish would be somewhere else.

Most of the boys in the town had had a go at catching flounders or dabs in the creeks or the harbour at low water, and there was always something to be caught, at least to make a breakfast or dinner; but they were always small, so there was no money to be made there. Old Ben explained to the two boys that they would never find worthwhile fish there in daylight, because then the big fish would be out at sea. The only place the odd big mature fish might be found, he said, was a certain creek that, before the draining of the Holkham marshes, used to flow up to the old harbour there. He thought that it might once have been an ancient spawning ground, which would account for the occasional mature fish there; but it was never more than one or two.

What the boys had to do, he said, was realise that the big fish came in at night, and then went back out to sea whenever the tide was right in the morning. To get a worthwhile catch they must be up at dawn with their lines baited and ready at the harbour mouth.

Getting up before light was no hardship for a gamekeeper's son who was used to work starting before the sun was up; so Pat and Young Ben laid their plans, acquired some old herrings for bait, borrowed a rowing boat from Pat's father on condition that they would be back by breakfast time, and set out in the dark before dawn the next time the tide was right.

They baited up their lines, old tackle they had scrounged, rowed to the harbour mouth, and laid out a line on each side of the boat. Then they waited, comfortable enough at first, warm from their long row, sitting and chatting quietly as the boat bobbed and swung on its anchor. But as the grey light of dawn replaced the almost cosy darkness it seemed to get much colder, young bodies began to chill, and enthusiasm for the life of a professional fisherman waned. Their lines, at first invisible in the darkness, began to show up against the dark water swirling past them, and they had the look of lines on the end of which absolutely nothing was happening. Young Ben had had enough, remarked casually that he would just check his bait, and began to haul in the cold, wet line with now frozen hands.

'Rotten thing's fouled on something,' he muttered. 'There must be a bit of wreck down there.' He hauled again. 'No,' he said with sudden excitement, 'it's alive!'

The first hook had a large, very lively flounder on it. So did the second. As the two boys, now very excited and oblivious to the cold water and the wild rocking of the little boat, hauled away at the line, every hook had a big threshing flat fish on it. Forgetting to unhook the lines carefully, they threw fish after fish into the bottom of the boat. Large fat plaice, worth good money at the fish dealer's, threshed about in the boat with an assortment of other saleable fish, and it was only after they had hauled in both lines, and the excitement had eased a little, that they realised what an entanglement of fish and lines they had made for themselves.

Then they had slowly and painstakingly to unhook each fish and untie a cat's cradle of knots in their tackle. But that done, they baited it up again and continued fishing, and as the dawn lit up the sea round them and the sun touched the tops of the sand-hills, they continued to haul fish out of the water. They rowed home with their catch, and had sold it within an hour of landing on the quay. Hurrah for the life of a bold fisherman!

After that success there was no stopping them, and for a time all thoughts were of what a time they were going to have, just fishing money out of the sea. But that particular ploy, which had worked so well for them, could only be repeated when the tide and weather were just right, so they had to think of something else.

Their first idea was to copy the professionals who went after the sea-trout with a long net along the shore. They didn't have the boat and equipment to go after the trout, but they did have a short bit of net they had scrounged, and reckoned that if they walked out to the shore at low water, they might well catch some more of these big fat flounders that had come so obligingly to their lines in the harbour.

They took Old Ben's advice as before, and he told them that it would be a waste of time except on a fine, warm day, with no wind, and at dead low water. 'Those big old 'uns like to feel the sun on their backs,' he said, 'but you won't catch them close inshore at any other time.'

Again the advice was good, and it worked. They trudged out over the sands on a suitable calm sunny day, carrying their net on a long pole between them. There Young Ben, who was the taller of the two, took one end of the net attached to the pole out as far as he could wade; then he turned, and leaning back until the water was up to his neck, he dragged the net along parallel with the beach. Pat, with his end of the net, kept pace with him just above where the sea lapped gently on the low water mark. Neither made a sound that might disturb a fish sunbathing in the shallows.

Success again. After a time Ben dragged his end of the net back into the shore, and as he hauled it up on to the beach a heaving and splashing began within the scope of the net as big flat-fish tried to escape back into deep water. They were able to fill the sack that they had hopefully brought with them, and soon sold their catch. Full of their cleverness, they were impatient to have another go, and the very next time Pat could get time off from helping his father, they were off over the sands again. But the weather wasn't quite the same. It was fine and sunny, but there was a bit of a breeze out of the nor'west. 'You're wasting your time, boy,' said Old Ben. But they were full of self-confidence and off they went. This time there was a little swell on the sea, and though they both tried taking the seaward end of the net, they couldn't keep their footing in deep water. They would get the net along a few yards, and then a gentle swell would lift the one at the deep end off his feet. The smooth, silent, deadly operation of the first attempt soon became just two boys splashing about in the sea. They caught hardly anything, and went home with just two or three dabs for breakfast, which they could probably have caught in the creeks in ten minutes. By ill chance Old Ben happened to be on the quay when they trudged wearily up from the beach carrying their pitiful catch and the heavy, soaking wet net on the pole between them; they tried to avoid him, but without success. He just glanced at the nearly empty sack and shook his head at them. 'You'll learn,' he said. 'You'll learn.'

Like all fishermen, they were learning that it is never as easy as it looks, but Old Ben took pity on them, and gave them some more advice from his apparent endless knowledge of fish and their ways.

There is a rather strange place between Wells and Blakeney, way out on the sand flats, only visible at low tide, called Warham Hole. Whichever way you approach it, it is a very long walk, and indeed probably only a few local people have ever seen it. It is a place where water ebbing away from the creeks has scored out a sort of big, deep pond in the beach, just above low water mark, and which even at dead low water always has several feet of water in it. Old Ben had studied this - he must have been as much a naturalist as fisherman - and knew that fish there behaved in a rather unusual way. He explained to the two lads that at night big fish would come in on the tide to feed on the beach and up the creeks, and that as the tide receded they would swim down towards the sea again, as you would expect. But then, if it was some time before dawn, some at least would stay in Warham Hole until the tide flowed again; then, as soon as the incoming tide reached them, they would swim on, back out to sea. He reckoned that if they were there before dawn on a day that would see the tide flowing in at daybreak, they could put their bit of net across the mouth of the hole and catch the big fish on their way out to the deep water.

Beginning to realise that successful fishing always seemed to involve a lot of hard work, and usually getting up in the middle of the night, Young Ben and Pat still decided to have a go. Having assured Pat's father again that he would be back by breakfast time, they made their plans and carried their net out again to the low water mark. A very long slog this time, over the marshes by way of many sheep bridges, stumbling through the mud and over the sands - all in the dark, of course. By the time they reached their objective there was just enough light over the open sand-flats to see where they were going, the eastern horizon was light grey and brightening, and the morning tide was creeping up the beach.

Quickly they pegged their net over the drain where Warham Hole, dark and sinister, ran into the sea, and made their final preparations. They would have to make sure the big fish, which they fervently hoped were really there, down in the black water somewhere, would move into their net before the incoming tide covered the whole area. There was only one way of ensuring that, and it meant taking their clothes off and going into the very cold and unwelcoming water themselves. They had brought sticks with them, and when the incoming tide reached the net they plunged into the dark pool at the far end, and beat the water as they made their way slowly along it towards their carefully arranged net.

Old Ben had got it right again, and this time they had more fish than they could carry all the way back to Wells, so they just picked out the biggest and let the others go back to the sea. But that was their last big fishing expedition. They realised that, brilliant as these schemes were, they would only work at particular times when the tides and all conditions were just right, and they would never earn more than an occasional handful of pocket money.

Pat knew that he would have to look elsewhere for anything like a really steady income.

—✤✦✤—

Chapter Six

Somehow that hoped-for state never seemed quite to arrive, but he kept looking and, as often happens to those who keep on looking, fate continued to throw the occasional remunerative job in his direction.

At that time trees were being planted on the sand dunes, part of the sea defence work that was always going on along the northern edge of the Holkham estate, and there were complaints about damage being done by the very healthy rabbit population. This came within Pat's father's domain, so the lad was given the chance to clear rabbits from the young trees, and make out of it what he could. Patrick had a friend to help, of course, and they soon made an arrangement with a butcher who said he would take all the rabbits they could trap.

Then night after night was spent on the sand-hills with a net; there were plenty of rabbits, and the few pence each that the butcher gave soon began to add up. At the time that Patrick was out at night rabbiting, he could still help his father during the day, so this arrangement went along quite happily for everybody.

The long autumn evenings grew short, afternoons became dark, but still rabbit-netting went on by the light of the moon. Young boys earning some regular money at last did not notice the cold, only the excitement of working amongst the dunes in the stark black and white shadows of the moonlight. When rabbiting was finished Pat had a few shiny, yellow sovereigns of his own, which he kept in a box under his bed; but then he had to find another job. Again it would have to be something that would still let him continue to help his father during the day; but with the spring came a new opportunity.

Several small boats worked out of Wells, netting the sea-trout. These were all four-man teams who, weather and tide permitting, would go out of the harbour in the evening, work just offshore all night, and return on the morning tide. One of these boats was owned by four old men, and one of them had decided that he had had enough of it, and so the other three had to find a new man to help. Patrick managed to persuade them that he could row and haul nets as well as anyone else, and they agreed to take him.

It was a hard way to earn a little money. He was young and strong, and ready to have a go at anything, but these old men had been fishing all their lives, and the sea was their home. Even on fine nights in good weather it was hard, hard work; rowing the heavy boat out of the harbour and along the shore, and then hauling the unwieldy, heavy nets for hours until it was time for the long row home again. Patrick was the butt of plenty of heavy-handed humour, as he struggled to pull his weight in this new environment. The worst part was often at the end of their fishing, when they were waiting for the tide to flow and take them over the bar and into the harbour again. The heavy old boat, piled to the gunwales with the soaking, lead-heavy nets, would wallow at anchor just outside the breaking surf on the shore line, while the three old men shared the only refreshment they ever took with them, a gallon can of beer. They would offer him a swig of it, and if he refused to swallow some they would gaze hard into his pale, greenish face thoughtfully and say that he didn't look very well, 'but never mind, he'll make a very handsome corpse.'

The young boy was all too well aware of the danger, apart from the sheer discomfort, of being in a small, heavily-laden open boat in those conditions. If a strong wind came up from the north while they were at sea, being close inshore was well recognised as being in a very dangerous position. A bigger craft would try to get well off-shore and ride it out, but all they could do was hope for the best and slip into the harbour the moment the tide rose high enough. Patrick used to take his boots off. He was a good swimmer, and had worked out that with bare feet he could just about swim ashore if he had to. It was better, he reasoned, to have cold feet than to drown. He was completely baffled by the fearlessness of the old men, who knew as well as anyone that fishermen sometimes do not come home from the sea, yet never seemed to worry about the danger at all. Whatever the conditions they took no account of them; and always wore thick leather, hob-nailed, thigh-length boots that no one could have swum a yard in.

Patrick did a few good trips with the old fishermen, but there still seemed to be little money in fishing. They gave him a few shillings to add to his little board, but they themselves seemed to make very little. On a bad night, and there were plenty of those, when there were no sea-trout, or the weather turned bad, it did not even pay for their can of beer. There were some good nights, when they came home with a good haul of dark silver trout to sell to the fish merchant; then there would be a good deal more ale drunk in the Royal Standard or Golden Fleece, but there seemed little chance of a young man becoming rich in the trade.

In due course the three old men found a permanent new member for their crew, and Patrick was not too sad to move on and look for other possibilities. He did a few trips with the whelk fishers, and did odd jobs round the busy port of Wells, but by the time he had reached his mid-teens he seemed to have tried everything, and thought perhaps he had better look again at keepering as a profession.

Being the son of a gamekeeper, he knew that the most important thing on the great estates was the number and quality of the game birds raised every year; and so he decided to be an expert on the raising of pheasants. At the same time, because of his father's position in that tight little world, he was well placed to get a job on one of the estates, and it happened that a dozen miles or so away from his home at Wells, an old keeper of great experience was on the point of retiring. He let it be known that he would consider letting young Patrick work with him to help to raise a thousand pheasants for the coming season. The young man reported for duty full of enthusiasm, which was just as well, as he soon found out that he was expected to do most of the work.

The first job he had to do was far from any glamorous notion he might have had of sauntering round with a gun, watching the young birds and potting at the odd marauding crow. He was shown piles of old dilapidated chicken coops, which he would have to refurbish and get ready for the hens that would sit on the pheasant eggs and mother the young birds. All that dusty work with hammer and nails completed, the next thing he was told was to get the rearing field ready. This was an enormous thirty-acre hay field; every inch of its hedges had to be inspected for signs of any sort of predator, and then secured by digging tunnels through the banks in which gin traps could be placed. An old hut on wheels was dragged into position by two horses; that would be his home while the birds had to be guarded closely. A large boiler was trundled along too, for preparing all the food the hens and eventually the young pheasants would need.

Now began a phase more pleasing to a young man – bird's-nesting on the grand scale. Every egg that was going to produce a pheasant had first to be found. For days nearly every daylight hour had to be spent searching hedgerow, spinney and wood for eggs. Sometimes as many as thirty eggs came from a single nest, as some hen pheasants seemed to have the convenient habit of congregating and all laying their eggs in the same place. What little time was left after this Patrick had to spend on his bike, going round farms in the neighbourhood looking for suitable sitting hens. Everybody kept hens in those days, and they were all the old-fashioned breeds that went broody regularly. A broody hen would be pretty useless unless you had a job for it, and the head keeper was in a position to offer a good price, so plenty were available. After the scout had gone round on his bicycle, his instructor would go round in a pony and trap, pay the going rate, and collect the sitting hens.

Back on the estate, each hen would be tried out with a nest of dummy eggs for a few days, and, if found to be a good steady sitter, would be put in one of the coops with a nest full of pheasants' eggs. The daily routine of looking after the hens and eggs then began in earnest, and young Patrick's job every morning at eight o'clock precisely was to visit each hen coop, gently extract the hen from her batch of eggs, and tether her a few yards away by a cord round one leg. She was then fed and watered, and encouraged to take a little gentle exercise before going back to her rather strange brood of eggs again. Hens never seemed to notice or care that they were sitting on some other bird's eggs; all a good broody hen wants to do is sit on eggs, any eggs. So they are smaller than usual, and spotted, who cares?

While eggs were being brooded, more work went on preparing the rearing field. The hardest job was scything the rapidly growing hay, which the old keeper and the young lad had to do with only one helper, and preparing rides in the grass at carefully-spaced intervals. When the eggs were hatched one coop with hen and pheasant chicks would be placed in each ride, so that the young birds would have short, dry grass to run about on. A wagon-load of coops moved slowly round the thirty-acre field while the spaces were measured up and prepared, and at every designated spot a coop was hauled down off the cart and arranged in its place. Water and feeding-bowls were put in place, and when all was ready a hen with her newly-hatched brood was carefully ensconced.

At this stage the young apprentice pheasant-rearer had to take up his residence in the field too, but that was a much less formal business. A straw mattress was placed in the hut on wheels, and that was it. It didn't worry him. He was well used to nights out on the marshes, and cooking his own breakfast; sleeping in a hut in a field, accompanied only by one thousand young pheasants and some hens, just went with the job.

By this time the feeding of the birds was in itself a big job for one young man. Grain and meal was provided by the estate, but the essential protein for a balanced diet consisted of rabbit carcasses cooked up in the big boiler, and they had to be obtained by walking round with a gun in the evening. No ready-mixed special feed for raising pheasants in those days; also an endless watch had to be kept for predators. Traps all round the field were inspected routinely, but even then an odd weasel might get in and take a chick. That, or the appearance of a sparrow-hawk, or perhaps a kestrel, in the sky overhead would drive the old keeper into paroxysms of rage. To him almost anything that was not a game bird or farm animal was vermin. His whole life had been dedicated to the running of a successful shooting estate, and to him a beautiful hawk hovering in the blue summer sky was just something that had to be got rid of as soon as possible. Usually they were soon tracked down to their nests and shot by one of the keepers, but the young man was kept too busy doing everything else to be involved in this, and he was glad of it.

He well knew that his job involved killing weasels or anything else preying on this great flock of young birds spread over the rearing field, but he had already decided that he did not like the wholesale persecution of hawks that was considered a matter of routine at that time. He was very observant of nature, and had noticed that their prey was much more likely to be a mouse or sparrow than a young pheasant. He knew that crows were great raiders of pheasant or partridge nests, and was ready to treat them accordingly, but for the hawks he had a grudging regard that was ahead of his time.

Pat did his season in the rearing field, learned a lot about what hard work it was, and was glad of his fourteen shillings a week, which was good pay for a young man in those days. But he never went on any further with the career of a gamekeeper. His father was a keeper, and his younger brother looked as if he was going to be one too, but Pat just wanted to be more independent, and work out his own future. For the moment that future had not arrived, so life went on at home much as before.

But he was a boy who never stopped observing life around him, and learning and tucking interesting information away in his memory. He was even beginning to learn a little about farming as he took a wider interest in the life inland of Wells; many years later he was able to write a fascinating description of how, in those days, the salt marshes were used for grazing large flocks of sheep. One man, with several very canny dogs, worked the whole complicated system, and he loved to watch those dogs.

In those days the marshes had been made accessible to sheep and men by bridges over the main creeks. Each of these bridges had a gate at the end, partly to control the sheep, but mainly to make counting possible as they passed through on their way home every evening. It was a daily ritual that Pat often watched if he happened to be about.

All day long those sheep would have been foraging and meandering freely over their section of the marsh, perhaps a mile square, until, as the sun slid down towards the western horizon and evening came on, the shepherd would arrive to take them home. He would drive down one of the farm tracks to the edge of the marsh in his cart, with dogs riding or trotting alongside, and one or two of the sheep would instantly stop feeding and look up. Neither he nor the dogs had to do anything at this stage; the alerted sheep would let out a bleat or two and others began to look up too, take in the situation, and move. They seemed to be moving at random at first, but that was because the marsh is a maze of small creeks, invisible at a distance. The sheep had to find their way round them all, and so had to set out in a dozen different directions, but they had done that all their lives, and knew the way. Soon, still without any action from man or dog, they were converging on the path that would lead to their particular gate.

By the time the shepherd was ready the dogs would have them

nicely lined up, and as he held the gate just wide enough for them to come through it, two at a time, they would be counted and on their way to the higher ground above the salt marshes. It was if one or two happened to be late for roll-call that the dogs really came into their own.

If a sheep was missing the cause was nearly always the same: it had got into one of the very narrow creeks, perhaps only a foot or so wide, and had become wedged or stuck up to its shoulders in the mud. So, at a word from their master, the dogs would set out and search each and every narrow, winding creek and gully. They knew the marsh just as well as the sheep, of course, and being a bit brighter, knew just where a missing sheep would most likely be. Soon an excited yapping would bring the shepherd to where the wretched animal was stuck, and then it would be hauled out, black with mud and reeking, to run and join its white and sweet-smelling companions on the high ground.

These bridges, built for the sheep, were very useful for others too, and were constantly used by the coastguards, and possibly by some men who had less proper reasons for being on the marsh. There was a coastguard watch house, in those days, on the seaward edge of the Wells marshes, looking over the sea and towards Morston and Blakeney harbours. That was an area where any amount of illegal coastal activity might be going on, far from prying eyes. The coastguards were constantly tramping back and forth by night where the sheep grazed by day, and another bridge, further out than any of the others, was built so that they could get right over the marsh to the seashore, and their lookout, at any state of the tide.

The bridges and sheep paths were often used by yet others too, not smugglers, but simply fishermen walking home; for in the days before there were engines in boats, if the wind dropped in the evening, as it often does, it was common for fishing boats to be beached and left on the shore miles away, while the crew walked home. Pat knew, too, that many a cold, weary fisherman called in at the coastguard hut and had a drink of something to help him on the long trek home.

At weekends too, the Wells Volunteers used to march out along the sheep paths, and over those same bridges, to their rifle range in the sand-hills. In short, there were probably more people about on the saltings in those days than there ever are now.

Then, one winter's night, the wind blew from the north, and the tide came up and took that last, furthest bridge away, and it was never rebuilt. Some of the dunes, where the coastguards' watch house used to be, were also washed away, and they decided to build a new lookout on the landward side of the saltings. And after that a day came when the Wells Volunteers marched away to do more serious shooting, far from the sand dunes and shore they knew, and slowly, over many years, all the other bridges fell into disuse. The sheep disappeared, or perhaps someone decided that it was no longer economically viable to keep them on the marshes; within his lifetime Pat saw the marshes revert at last to the unfrequented wilderness that they had been before he was born. The scene of much activity was empty and quiet again, but for the noisy seagulls who nest there in the spring, and the muted greens and blues of the salt marsh were no longer broken by the myriad white blobs that were foraging sheep.

Chapter Seven

The years at the beginning of the twentieth century, that led up to the first world war, were not easy ones at Wells, but Pat and his young friends hardly noticed this as children. Everyone they knew seemed to be short of money and glad to scrounge a shilling here and there, but that was just the way things were, and their simple, hardy, life was natural and enjoyable to them. It was only as they began to grow up that they started to notice that regular, well-paid work was difficult to find

Wells had been a busy little port in its heyday, with as many as four pilots fully occupied, its harbour full of ships, and plenty of work for any strong young lad. However, by the time Pat was in his teens the coastwise trade had fallen off to such a degree that only one pilot remained, and even the steam tugboat had been reduced to trawling for fish. Stores and warehouses on the quay stood empty, and young men were steadily leaving the town to look for work elsewhere. Pat could always do work for his father, which provided him with a roof and food, but little cash. Ben, who was a couple of years older, had become a naval reservist, but they needed something more than that. They had noticed that the only people around with real money seemed to be the few 'gentlemen gunners' who were visiting the area more and more, and they decided there might be a good future in becoming professional guides.

Some of the longshoremen and fishermen were beginning to do this, in a casual sort of way, and stories about these visitors were current in the quayside bars, like the tale of the gentleman gunner who went shooting without a guide, in the fog.

This man had arrived from London one evening on the train, to shoot geese, he said. A local gunner had offered his services as guide, but these were turned down; the visitor said he was an expert shot, and would need no help. He obviously knew the rudiments of the sport for he got up early next morning, left his hotel for the sand-hills about dawn, and picked himself a likely spot to get a shot at a goose flighting over to the feeding grounds. As luck would have it, he picked on the very spot that the gunner whose help he had scorned usually favoured himself for the morning flight. This local man came along a few minutes later, saw a stranger there, and walked on thoroughly disgusted to a different spot a hundred yards away.

By this time, as often happens in autumn, a bit of a mist was collecting at ground level, and the two men were completely out of sight of each other. Suddenly a single goose appeared, out of range for the local man and flying towards the stranger. A double shot rang out, and moments later a goose fell out of the mist and landed beside the local gunner. It lay there stone dead on the sand, and nothing else happened. No more shots were fired, though there were several gunners dotted about the sand-hills and, after waiting in vain for someone to come and claim the goose lying beside him on the ground, the local man decided he might as well have it himself, fired into the air, picked up the goose, and put it in his bag. There was no further activity, and half an hour later the various shooters were all making their way back to Wells along the sea wall.

As two or three of them were talking, the stranger came up and, seeing that one of them had a goose, asked if it was for sale. 'Well,' said the local gunner, quick as a flash, 'I really need this one for a special order to go up to London, but I suppose if you could go sixpence above the usual price we could have a deal.' The goose changed hands, and they all set off again walking up to the town.

A few steps further on the visitor suddenly said, 'Dash it, the thing is, I know I've really got a brace to take home now, because I shot one out there on the beach, but I couldn't see it in the fog. I'm not going without it. I'm going back.' And off he strode back into the thickening fog. He was not seen again until he turned up at lunch time at the hotel, where he spent the rest of the day telling anyone who would listen about the bird that he knew he had killed, but that had completely disappeared. 'I know it was dead, I know it was dead,' he kept muttering. The story went all round the town, and kept people laughing for weeks, but he apparently never realised that he had shot a goose, then bought it - at sixpence above the usual price - and then spent several hours wandering round in the mist, carrying it and looking for it at the same time.

Many a local man had been earning the odd sovereign, acting as guide to guests who were staying at the town hotel, and Pat saw no reason why this could not be developed into something of a career. His father owned two houseboats, so why could not he and Ben fit out one of them as a sort of floating hotel, accommodate rich visitors, take them shooting, charge them a good whack, and soon become prosperous? They worked out between them the duties, such as ferrying guests and stores out in the dinghy, cooking and domestic chores aboard, guiding and tuition for the gentlemen shooters, but there were difficulties: neither of them had a gun or any proper equipment, and Pat's father had to be persuaded to let them use one of the houseboats.

The houseboat turned out to be easier than expected. Tom readily agreed to let them use one of his boats to try out their idea. He probably knew more about the local shooting scene than anyone else, and guessed that they might indeed make a little money out of it. He also let them use some of his gear to equip the houseboat; but they still had to obtain guns somehow, and they had very little money. However, they had good luck.

One morning, when they were out in the sand-hills rabbiting very early, they noticed that one or two empty, but brand new, barrels had been washed up on the shore; such things are always worth finding and they went to inspect them. Then they noticed more a bit further along the edge of the sand-hills, and then more, and realised that a deck load must have been washed off a passing ship during the night.

Later, they heard that this was exactly what had happened. There had been a stiff nor'easterly blowing, and a steamer bound for Yarmouth with a load of new barrels for the salt herring fishery there had lost his deck cargo. Ben and Tom were beside themselves with delight; this was serious salvage.

They spent the rest of the day collecting barrels, piling them

together, and writing their names in the sand as proof of ownership, then making them into rafts, and over several tides rowing them up to the quay. Soon others, always ready for a bit of scrounging, were looking for their share in the salvage money, and hot disputes broke out, but the two lads managed to get a hundred and twenty barrels to the Customs Officer at Wells, and were awarded £6 salvage money - as much as they might have taken several weeks to earn any other way. This was a breakthrough, for Pat knew where there was an old, but apparently sound, twelve-bore shotgun that could be bought for £2.

He had seen it standing, rusty and neglected, in the corner of the butcher's slaughterhouse in the town, and had been told it was for sale. An apparently casual inspection told him that all the working parts still functioned, and as soon as he had his share of the salvage money, he put in his bid, which was accepted. He still had to get a gun licence, however, to carry it in the street outside, so his next stop was the post office. It was necessary to be very punctilious about this because he knew full well that the same old policeman who had been the butt of him and his friends in former years was still about, and would be delighted to catch him carrying a gun without a licence.

Pat spent a few more of his scarce shillings in the post office, and then, complete with licence, went back to the slaughterhouse and picked up his new property. He could now perfectly legally carry his gun under the nose of the officer of the law; having noticed him down the street gazing idly in a shop window, he shouldered his gun in military style and, whistling a rousing march, strode ostentatiously down the middle of the road past his old enemy. An officious cry of 'What are you doing with that gun without a licence, you young varmint?' was all Pat wanted to make his joy complete, but it was not to be.

The old policeman knew those boys better than they knew themselves, and he was not going to be caught out with that one; having previously noticed Pat going into the post office, he had put two and two together. He observed, reflected in the shop window, the military pantomime going on behind him, and did not even turn his head, then he sauntered on up the street while a slightly crestfallen youth, no longer whistling, went on his way home with his rusty twelve-bore.

Ben and he spent the rest of that day cleaning the old gun up, and then took it on the marshes to try shooting its 'pattern' into a convenient mud bank. It was better than they had expected and, inspired by this success, Ben also had soon acquired an even older shotgun from a farmer he worked for from time to time. This weapon had been used for many years as a crow-scarer, and had worse problems than a coat of rust. They took it to the blacksmith, a shooting man himself, and he did what he could to tighten it up and make it safe to use. It still needed a piece of elastic to hold the breech lever in the correct position, but it was probably no worse than some of the ancient fowling pieces that other longshore men used; they felt they were almost ready to start business.

The two young men, no longer mere boys, worked hard to get the houseboat ready, and by the time a new shooting season started in September they had only to find clients. The boat was kitted out with bunks and bedding, fuel for the coal stove, paraffin for the lamp, and a cask of fresh water. There had been plenty of ribbing and chat on the waterfront about their new career as floating hotel owners; everyone knew about it and soon one of the visiting would-be gunners at the hotel contacted them and asked about terms and conditions. They had decided that living aboard the houseboat would be free, but guests would have to pay for guiding, tuition, and their food. This was readily agreed upon, and they were soon ferrying their first customer out in the dinghy.

It was a fine autumn, and still too warm for serious shooting, but their client, a schoolteacher, did not seem to mind. He said he just enjoyed being aboard, and the rough and ready life, the food, which consisted mainly of fried mutton chops, and tramping over the marshes in the fine autumnal weather. Since there was little shooting, they took him fishing instead, and he loved it all. At the end of the two weeks he had booked up for, they rowed him and his gear back to the quay, and he insisted on paying more than they asked. This was indeed the life. Pat and Ben soon had the houseboat cleaned up and ready for their next guest, with stores refurbished, and an added case of ships' biscuits to tide them over occasions when nobody remembered to go to the baker's to get some bread.

Their next customer turned out to be a major in the army, who also seemed to enjoy the simple life on board the houseboat, the hard bunks and the rather basic diet; but they learned in conversation that he had been gold-prospecting in Alaska in his youth, and probably found life on the salt marshes almost cosy. Where he had been, he used to tell them, if you tried to make tea by pouring boiling water into the teapot, by the time it hit the tea leaves it was solid ice.

He was married to the daughter of a rich family in London, and was probably delighted to get away from society life for a couple of weeks. There was still little shooting weather, but he enjoyed himself, he said, just seeing the skeins of geese flying high overhead, and going for walks along the shore at low tide. They only managed to get two or three ducks in the course of his stay, but he shot a pink-foot goose the day before he had to return to London, and expressed himself well satisfied.

The houseboat crew decided that this was almost too easy a way of making a living, but with their next client they learned, like every other hotel proprietor ashore or afloat, that there are good guests and the other sort.

The Hon. Frederick Something-or-other, as he was always remembered, sent them a message that their houseboat had been recommended to him and he would spend a week with them for the shooting. Ben took the dinghy up to the quay at the time arranged to meet him, and found the Hon. Frederick standing there with a hotel porter and a mound of luggage on a trolley. Ben was used to handling the odd battered suitcase, but his jaw

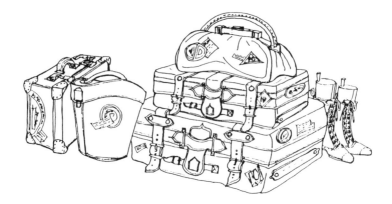

dropped at the sight of this small mountain of highly-polished leather. Still, determined to do his best, he somehow managed to get it all aboard, helped by the smirking porter and the would-be sportsman, and very carefully rowed the grossly-overloaded dinghy the long mile up the creek to where the houseboat lay at anchor. It was already quite clear, from the nervous way the Hon. Frederick was looking about him at the water swirling past only a couple of inches below the gunwale, that this was not quite the sporting venue he had expected.

At the houseboat, it was Pat's turn to hide his horror at the sight of the dinghy approaching, apparently sinking under a load of expensive baggage, with a rigid gentleman sitting in the stern, and Ben trying his best to bring it up to the houseboat without water coming in over the side and sending them straight to the bottom. Leaning out as far as he could, Pat grasped their bow-rope and very carefully brought them alongside, while Ben equally gingerly somehow managed to bring the oars inboard amongst the luggage; they both knew that one false move would see the dinghy flooded, the shiny suitcases floating away, and everyone very wet. Luckily, the passenger was too petrified by this time to do anything as rash as to move about; so Pat was able to somehow get a firm grip on him where he sat, and with great care managed to hoist him aboard. That done, the luggage soon followed, and was stowed away under bunks and in the tiny forepeak.

Having given the new guest plenty of time to adjust to his new surroundings, Pat explained that with the tide going out they would soon be able to walk over the marsh to the shore, and might get a shot at geese on the evening flight. 'Ah,' said the guest, 'I shall need this then.' He opened one of the shiny cases and produced a smart leather-covered thermos flask, which he handed to them. 'Coffee, not tea.'

Pat, the guide, passed this to Ben, the cook, who bemusedly heated up some coffee on the stove and filled it. Pat next advised donning suitable clothes and boots. The guest produced a pair of leather ankle-boots, of the type that would be worn for a fine day's pheasant-shooting. Pat, embarrassed, tried to explain that these were not suitable for trudging through mud and sea water; but then the difficult situation was resolved by the Hon. Frederick suddenly deciding that he would not go shooting just then. It was beginning to get dusky outside the houseboat, and he really preferred shooting when he could see where to put his feet. He had given the matter some attention, he said, and he felt it would really be much better to go shooting in the morning. 'We can have a quiet evening in,' he said, 'because it is really not very nice outside, and after dinner you can tell me what interesting local stories you know.'

The two young men looked at each other. Local stories? Who had said anything about telling stories? Still, if the paying customer wanted stories...

'Pat here does stories,' said Ben. 'I'll be getting on with dinner.'

'What stories?' hissed Pat as they clattered about getting a meal together.

'Tell him about them three girls.'

Although they guessed that something more ambitious for dinner was expected, their knowledge of cookery being what it was, and their shipboard stores being what they were, they just produced their standard shooters' repast, and it was soon on the table. This consisted, as always, of fried mutton chops and gravy, bread and jam, and cocoa. It had always gone down well with their clients so far, when they staggered back to the houseboat after long tramps over saltings and shore. The one who had been prospecting in Alaska even declared with great relish that the smell reminded him of the good old days of his youth. Their present guest did not say what it reminded him of, and his general attitude suggested nothing very pleasant, but he ate it with reasonably good grace. Being a public school boy, he had probably known worse.

After dinner Ben and Pat made the washing up and tidying the cabin last as long as possible, but it was obvious that their guest was waiting for the entertainment to begin, so at last they had to sit down on one side of the little table, while he sat on the other, looking at them expectantly. Ben also looked at Pat, and Pat, after fishing about in his pockets, brought out a dog-eared packet of Woodbines, which turned out to have only one cigarette in it. The Hon. Frederick produced an expensive cigarette case from his breast pocket and tentatively offered it round; they both accepted the offer, and lit up in their usual manner at the lamp. He solemnly tapped his on the pigskin case, and then lit it from a tiny silver vestas box. They all drew appreciatively at the fine tobacco, and then looked at each other. Seeing no hope for it, Pat said, 'Well, there's this story about these three girls, and that's a rum old story, I can tell you.' He did not really think it was much of a mystery himself, but it was talked about for years, especially amongst visitors, and had acquired a slight smack of the supernatural.

'My dad,' said Pat, 'knew all about it because he was probably the last person to see them. They were three young women, not little girls, and they were here for a day's outing. They came from some village inland, but I forget where that was; anyhow they were to have a day by the seaside. They were round all the shops in the morning, and a lot of people in the town remembered seeing them. But then nobody thought any more about it until the next day, when the word suddenly got about that they had not got home on their train and they were saying they must be lost, but no one knew how they could have got lost in a little town like Wells.

'Now it just happened that my dad had seen them walking on the beach that afternoon, at low water, but he hadn't thought anything about that because that was a nice day, and though there weren't as many visitors then as there are now, it wasn't that unusual to see people walking along the shore on a warm summer's day. Anyhow, when he heard that they were lost, he told the coastguard, and of course he laughed and said, "Well, they are not likely to be still walking, unless they can't find their way up the beach road, but I'll go and have a look round."

'Of course, they might have got lost in the sand-hills somehow, and wandered off in the wrong direction, towards Holkham or something. But how could they disappear for so long? Well, people soon began to think up all sorts of things about what might have happened to these girls, and everyone was talking about it and guessing this or that might have happened. But then, as soon as a proper search started, they were found straight away. There they were on the beach, not far from where my dad had seen them the day before. But they were all stone dead. Not a mark on them, they said, all dressed up in their going-out frocks, but dead all right, and soaked through. Well, of course, the tide had been in and gone out again twice.

'Well, no one knew what to make of that. If they had drowned on the beach, how could they still be in the same place after two tides? And still all together? There was a real old to-do then. The police came from all over the place to investigate, but what could they possibly know about it? People got to saying that it must have been quicksands that got them, and they all stuck there until the tide came and drowned them. But I never heard that there were any quicksands on the beach there. Quicksands come and go in the channels on big tides, of course, but not on the beach like that.'

'So, what had happened to the poor girls, then?' his one-man audience wanted to know, probably hoping for a dramatic ending to the tale.

'That's the funny thing,' said Pat. 'No one ever knew. Mind

you, I think they just walked down to the edge of the sea at low water, and the tide came in behind them. That could easily happen if you didn't know what you were doing. The beach is all little channels that fill up quickly when the tide flows. They didn't know that. They probably thought they could just paddle across somewhere. You can just imagine them having a bit of a laugh and then with them long dresses and stuff they got into trouble, and before they knew what was happening they would be out of their depths. I bet they just drowned, and by pure chance the bodies all washed up together; the sea does stranger things than that.'

'Is that the story, then?' said the Hon. Frederick, apparently rather disappointed, and perhaps not really in the mood for tales of drownings.

'Well,' said Pat, 'that's what happened, and I can tell you there was a lot of fuss about that, and people still talk about it, and they say that there was something really strange about them girls dying there on the beach.'

'But you don't think there was anything supernatural about it, do you?'

'Well,' said Pat again, beginning to feel that he had not struck the right note, 'no, I don't say I think that myself, though some do. But if you want to hear about a real true ghost story, there's the Hanging Tree up behind the town.'

'Does anyone drown?' asked his audience.

'No,' said Pat. 'There's this place up behind the town, isn't there Ben? You won't catch anyone there after dark.' Ben nodded; he knew the old tale well enough.

'Well,' said Pat, feeling he was getting all the hard work, 'there is this place, at the back end of the town, if you go up Market Lane and just keep going; not that there is anything much there now, except a long lane that goes up the hill to the lodge at the top. That used to be called Gallows Hill, and long ago, before they took murderers and the like to Norwich to hang them, they used to take them up there. Well, the story is that one day there was to be a hanging on the gallows at the top of the hill, and no doubt the hangman and all the officials were waiting there, and these other men were taking this chap up there from the gaol. So off they went, climbing up this little old path, and it was a hot day, and it is a steep path.

'So they got as far as a sort of thicket, about halfway up the hill, and these men were all as drunk as lords. I suppose they had to get them drunk, to get them to do a job like that on a hot day. Or any day, I suppose. Anyhow, when they had got there, they decided they didn't want to go any further, so they just took this chap, and they hung him then and there from an old tree, and they just left him, and went back to the pub, I suppose.' Pat paused, wishing he had a bit more of a story to tell. 'Well, that's about it. But there's a ghost there all right, and they say it's this old chap still a-swinging on that old tree. No one goes up there at night, I can tell you. That's right, isn't it Ben?'

'Yes,' said Ben. Then, feeling he should add a bit more support, 'Yes. That's right, no one'll go up there at night, I can tell you.'

'I'm not surprised to hear it,' said the Hon. Frederick, probably feeling that he had not struck a very fruitful source of amusing country tales. 'Look, I think I'll turn in now. Be bright and fresh for the morning, what?'

But long after the smokey paraffin lamp had been blown out and the boys had climbed into their cosy bunks and had felt the tide come in again and lift the houseboat off its muddy berth, their paying guest could be heard shifting about uneasily. Although the boat rocked ever so gently at its anchor, he did not seem to be having a very good night's sleep, and probably did not really appreciate the soothing motion of the floating boat, the gurgling of flowing water and the night noises of the saltings.

The next day he showed little enthusiasm for the morning flight, and the very idea of hunting the wild goose seemed to have lost its magic. When Pat tried to give him some good advice about getting proper boots, he suddenly announced that he had rather decided against wildfowling as a sport. He thought perhaps the life would not suit him, and if they would row him back to the quay, he would call it a day.

So they packed him and all his luggage in the dinghy again, and took him back. But he did still pay up for the whole week as contracted, so Pat and Ben reckoned that they had not done too badly over the deal, and had many a laugh over it. But they agreed there and then that in future they would make it plain to customers that the price did not include after-dinner entertainment.

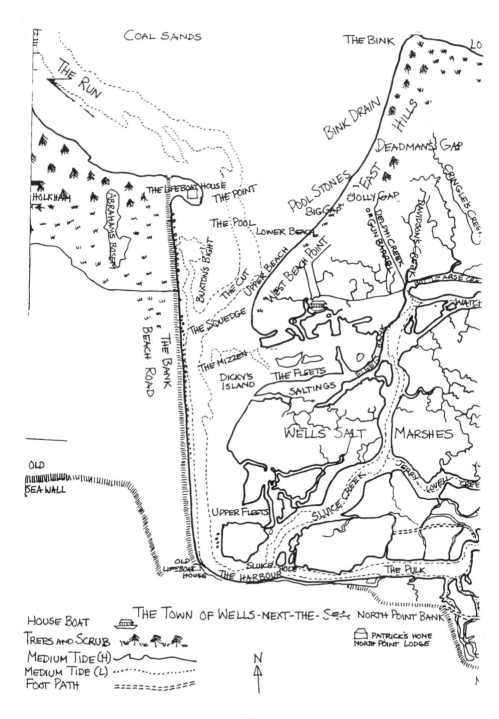

COAL SANDS THE BINK LO

THE RUN

THE LIFEBOAT HOUSE THE POINT BINK DRAIN EAST HILLS

DEADMANS GAP

HOLKHAM ABRAHAMS BOSOM POOL STONES JOLLY GAP CRINGLE'S CREEK

THE POOL BIG GAP

LOWER BEACH DELPHI CREEK DAVIDSON'S CREEK

THE CUT UPPER BEACH OR GUN BARREL

BURTONS BIGHT WEST BEACH POINT BILLY ARSE CREEK

BEACH ROAD THE BANK THE SQUEDGE WATCH

THE MIZZEN

DICKY'S ISLAND THE FLEETS

SALTINGS

WELLS SALT MARSHES

OLD SEA WALL

JERRY LOVELL CREEK

UPPER FLEETS SLUICE CREEK

OLD LIFEBOAT HOUSE SLUICE HOLE THE PULK

THE HARBOUR

NORTH POINT BANK

HOUSE BOAT

THE TOWN OF WELLS-NEXT-THE-SEA

TREES AND SCRUB

PATRICK'S HOME
NORTH POINT LODGE

MEDIUM TIDE (H)

MEDIUM TIDE (L)

FOOT PATH

N

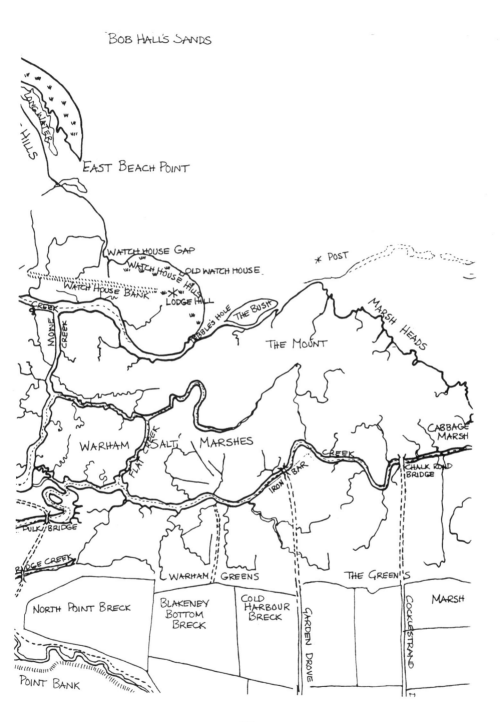

BOB HALL'S SANDS

LONGWATER HILLS

EAST BEACH POINT

WATCH HOUSE GAP

WATCH HOUSE HILLS   OLD WATCH HOUSE

* POST

WATCH HOUSE BANK

LODGE HILL

PEBBLES HOLE

THE BUSH

MARSH HEADS

CREEK

MORE CREEK

THE MOUNT

CABBAGE MARSH

WARHAM   SALT   MARSHES

FLAT CREEK

CREEK

IRON BAR

CHALK ROAD BRIDGE

PULK BRIDGE

BRIDGE CREEK

WARHAM   GREENS

THE GREENS

MARSH

NORTH POINT BRECK

BLAKENEY BOTTOM BRECK

COLD HARBOUR BRECK

GARDEN DROVE

COCKLESTRAND

POINT BANK

Chapter Eight

After a time the houseboat, run for visiting gunners by Pat and Ben, became well known, and had its own regular clientèle. There was Charles, the local blacksmith who had helped them fix that first shotgun that Ben acquired from the farmer; there was Jeffrey, a London solicitor who, from being a casual visitor, became a close friend; and there was Frank, a professional artist who had moved to Wells.

As time went on, Ben was less often at the houseboat. He had married and felt in need of more regular income, or perhaps his wife told him he did, a young wife not being too happy about the idea of her new husband going off to spend his nights on a houseboat on the saltings. At all events, Ben turned more towards a new and steady business that was starting up along the coast, that of providing bait for the amateur fishermen who were coming to the east coast more and more. The job of digging worms for baiting their lines was hard, and dull compared to the old houseboat, but the income from it was quite good, and very regular.

Pat continued taking on paying guest gunners in the season, and other jobs in the summer, often working with Frank, who illustrated books and articles for magazines that had to do with shooting and the country life. Many a brilliant illustration of wildfowlers shooting geese over the marshes was composed with the help of Pat, acting as the model, and also arranging a dead bird craftily strung on wires, in a suitably artistic posture. Frank in his turn often helped with the houseboat when Ben was not there.

The attraction of the houseboat for visiting gentlemen gunners had been increased by the addition of two gun-punts. The first had originally belonged to Pat's father, who had done some professional wildfowling in his youth, and it had lain unused for years until Ben and Pat had taken it over. They spent many hours working on it and bringing it up to a suitable state to be used by their guests, but it was a single punt for carrying one person, and they soon realised that a double punt would be much more useful. Few of their customers had the slightest idea how to use such a craft by themselves, and come back alive.

Jeffrey, the lawyer, also rather fancied the idea of being able to use a double punt, and asked Pat to see how much it would cost to get one built. There was little chance of buying a second-hand one, such things being fairly uncommon, and probably in constant use by any professional wildfowler who happened to have one. One of the boat builders at Wells, without a lot of work on his hands, said he would build a punt for them for £8, unpainted. Everybody agreed this was very reasonable, so it was built, painted up, and otherwise got ready by Ben and Pat, and was soon in use.

In truth, it never did great slaughter amongst the geese, as it might have done in the hands of a professional. Where a serious wildfowler, who depended for his living on the number of geese he could send to market, would have spent all night in deadly earnest stalking birds at rest on the sand banks or the shallows, the houseboat gun punts were used more for the entertainment of the visitors. It was an exciting business for someone who had never experienced it before, to crouch in the front of the double punt as it was propelled silently over the dark sea towards a group of swimming geese. It could only be done at all when the moon, the tide, and the weather were just right.

Geese, whatever the time of night, are wide awake to anything unusual, and it was an almost impossible task to ease the dark shape of the gun punt silently towards them, without them sensing it. Nearly always, just as some geese were almost within range, clearly visible as dark shapes on the grey water, one would suddenly stick his head straight up, begin to make loud, suspicious noises, and they would all abruptly change direction and swim

away. But no one was too worried about this sort of end to a long stalk. Most of the paying guests were thrilled by the mere experience.

Few people, then as now, have the chance of stalking wild geese between dark sky and dark sea, with perhaps just a glint of moonlight glancing between clouds to illuminate the still water and the distant sand-hills. No sound but the far and faint noises of the open sea, and the even more distant, thin noises of the countryside beyond the marshes: perhaps the far-away yap of a farm dog, somewhere inland, but close at hand only the gentle lapping of the sea, inches from where you crouch in your gun punt. It was an experience to be remembered and boasted about, and if the visitor could also carry, so nonchalantly, just one grey goose with his shooting gear on his journey home, that was enough.

One of Pat's friends was particularly keen to see what the double punt could do. He was a man who seemed to spend most of his time thinking about wildfowling, always kept a gun at his place of work, and was well known for grabbing it and running outside whenever the wild geese flew over. Whatever he happened to be doing at the time, if the geese seemed to him to be going in a promising direction, he would leave everything, and rush off after them. Sometimes he managed to bag a goose, and sometimes he did not; perhaps he did not really care much, the hunt was the thing.

He was not a nautical man, and he did not care much about boats, but the idea of being able to get near a whole flock of geese fascinated him. So, soon after the double punt came into use he persuaded Pat to let him have a go on the first occasion possible when the moon and tide were right.

The day and the moment arrived, and on a suitable evening they left the houseboat in the double punt at about half flood, and set out through the creeks as the moon rose, aiming to arrive at the marsh heads just before high water. From there, on a big tide, they could move out from the marshes over the wide sands towards the open sea, where flocks of geese could be found swimming and chattering amongst themselves before setting out to fly inland to their chosen feeding ground. Timing was the great thing, and success or failure depended on being there at the right moment. On this occasion they seemed to have arrived just too late, for by the time the tide allowed them to get to the right position the moon was getting higher in the sky and bunches of geese were already taking off and flying inland.

Pat suggested that the best thing would be for them to stay where they were, just outside the marsh heads, and wait quietly to see if any of the remaining geese swam towards them. They floated there on the still surface of the water for some time, listening to the geese and seeing parties of them flying inland, sometimes almost over their heads; but it didn't look as if they were going to get a shot with the punt gun. His companion, who had also brought his twelve-bore with him, just in case, wanted to have a go at some of the geese flying over; that would be the end of any idea of stalking with the punt, of course, but Pat agreed, in their whispered consultation, that he might as well have a go.

The very next time some geese drifted near to them, then took to the air and seemed to be within range, Pat said, 'Have a go then!' and he leapt to his feet in the punt and threw his twelve-bore up to his shoulder. One of the geese was swinging round towards them and he drew a bead on the great black bird - geese look very big close to, especially in the moonlight - then put one foot back to steady himself. But his foot missed the afterdeck of the punt and he stepped back into the sea. There was a great splash as he disappeared under water, then reappeared again sparkling in the moonlight, water cascading off him like some monster from the depths, and still holding his gun up in the air.

The sea, over the high sands, was only a couple of feet deep, and he stood there spluttering and gasping while Pat calmly drew the punt alongside, took the twelve-bore out of his hands, and emptied the cartridges from it into the bottom of the punt. Then he scrambled aboard again, and they started laughing.

That was the end of any possibility of shooting a goose that night, and the main thing was to get the would-be goose hunter, soaked to the skin as he was in near icy sea water, back to the houseboat as quickly as possible. It would have been a long slow trip back through the creeks against the now ebbing tide, so they took the punt as near as they could get to the open beach, left her anchored there to be collected later, and walked back through the sand-hills and over the marshes. Ben was there that night, and luckily had a good fire blazing away in their cabin stove; so they spent most of the rest of the night drying soaking clothes out as well as they could.

The houseboat gang often had a laugh about the events of that great goose-hunt, but out of sympathy for the victim no one else was ever told about his dramatic backwards dive into the sea, for which consideration he often expressed his gratitude.

—✦✦✦—

Pat's elder brother Jack had left home to see a bit of the world some years before these events, had ended up in America, married a farmer's daughter named Elizabeth, and was living in a remote part of the United States. In the early spring, a couple of years before the first world war, he wrote home and suggested that young Pat might like to go and visit him. He said he would like to hear all the news from Wells, and even offered to pay the steamer fare out, but cautiously added that his little brother would have to pay his own fare home again. Perhaps he thought that Pat would decide to stay out there too.

It was just that time of year when the shooting was all over and, with the last of the paying guests gone, there was a lot of time to be filled in before the season started again in the autumn. Pat had been looking round, without much enthusiasm, for some way to fill in the summer months, and soon decided that a trip abroad might be just the thing. After all, if brother Jack had managed to gain a wife and a farm so easily, who could know what America might have in store for him? He wrote back that he would have to be back in Wells for the new season in October, but that he would be on his way as soon as a passage had been arranged.

The White Star liner *Arabic* deposited him at the port of New York, where his brother met him off the ship, and they were soon on their way north. Jack and his American wife lived not far south of the Canadian border, in the foothills of the Adirondack mountains, a few miles from the little town of Fort Ann. Pat was impressed by New York, and by the long journey up the Hudson River valley to Schenectady, and then another fifty miles beyond that through what seemed to him a complete wilderness, up towards the mountains. Pat had never seen wild country and forests like this before, on a completely different scale to the countryside he was used to, and the final road from Fort Ann to the farm he would hardly have regarded as a decent cart-track. Without the reassuring presence of his brother, he would have begun to doubt if he would ever find his way home again.

Conditions on the farm were very basic, buildings all of wood, heated by a stove in the middle of the room, but Pat was not too worried - life had been even more primitive on the old houseboat. Jack seemed to have acquired an American accent, and his wife's was very strange to poor Pat at first, but they soon got used to each other. He had the knack of getting on with other people, and had acquired a certain familiarity with strangers from the houseboat visitors, that was probably unusual in a young man from the depths of the country in those days.

He soon buckled down to life on the farm, and helped with the unfamiliar crops. When they were not working there was hunting in the forest and fishing in the mountain streams. It was all about as different to life at home as you were likely to find: mountains instead of low sand-hills, different crops, different trees, different birds and beasts, even different fish in the fast, sparkling waters of the rivers where Jack took him fishing.

Time passed pleasantly, though Pat could not get used to there being no salt marsh outside the door, and when you stopped to think about it, the enormous distance from the sea was strange and almost frightening. He had never known a place before where the sea was more than just out of your range of vision. Norfolk tugged at the corner of his mind all the time, and one day when he happened to find an old Colman's Mustard tin that someone had discarded, he knew that he must soon go back. Well, he had said from the outset that he would be back in October, hadn't he?

He had also said that he would pay his fare home, and that presented a problem, for there was little chance of his earning much money in the Adirondack mountains. But there was a lot of work going on down in the valley a few miles from the homestead, where a canal was being dug. They had heard the noise of blasting and seen great machines slicing their way along when they had passed that way, and they had heard that there was a shortage of labourers.

One day Pat went off down the valley to see what the chances of work were, and soon found himself engaged as a pick and shovel man and general dogsbody. He worked on the canal site for several weeks and got together the cash for his return journey; he also managed to learn a little about the rudiments of canal-building. It was his nature to take an interest in whatever was going on, and though he had no idea then that it would ever be useful to him, he even acquired a little basic knowledge of the use of explosives as the engineers blasted out rock from the canal bed. No one dreamed then that, in a year or two, such knowledge would be at a premium in the trench warfare that was about to engulf Europe.

By October Pat had bought his return ticket and said goodbye to Jack and Elizabeth and his new friends, and was on his way back across the Atlantic again. Within a day of arriving back at Wells he and Frank were out with their guns in the sand-hills, and a day or two later Jeffrey arrived from London. Pat sank back into the old familiar, small-scale life of Norfolk, and the big, wide, new world of mountains and forests and canal-digging faded like a dream. The new houseboat season was soon under way, and they were busier than ever with visitors. Pat saw no reason why this life should be interrupted again; but the next time they toasted the new year it was 1914, and everybody's life was about to change.

Chapter Nine

Soon, all the talk was of war with Germany. By August, war was a fact. Meetings were being held all over the country calling for volunteers for the army, and young men, whom Pat knew, were enlisting. Ben, being a naval reservist, had already been called, and Pat felt he should go too but was undecided whether to join him, or go for the army. Then he heard that a Sportsmen's Battalion was being formed and when he went to talk to his friend Frank about it he found that he, in spite of being over forty years old, was thinking of joining too. Pat told him that he was far too old to be a soldier, and would never be able to keep up with the young men, even if they would have him, but Frank wouldn't take that. 'What have I got to fear about route marches with a lot of young boys,' he said, 'when I have spent my time marching and scrambling over sand-hills and saltings at night, when they, dear little souls, have been safely tucked up in bed?' Pat knew there was little chance of dissuading him, and, sure enough, soon after Pat had taken his medical, been accepted, and arrived at the battalion's head-quarters in London, Frank turned up too

The Sportsmen's Battalion was filling up fast as, in the spirit of those times, sportsmen from all over Britain answered the call for soldiers to fight for their country. There was none of the cynicism then that people were to come to feel about war and patriotism. A war against Germany was seen by many as a sort of grand sporting fixture, to decide who would be champion of Europe. In Pat's company, as it took shape and they began training at the beginning of 1915, were gamekeepers and ghillies, footballers and golf professionals, sportsmen of one sort or another from all walks of life, including, Pat noticed, a member of Parliament and a clergyman.

They began by having time on their hands in the big city, with a certain amount of marching about, but nothing much to do in the evenings; Pat had soon got rid of the little money he had brought with him and, like most of these young countrymen, was at a loose end in London. But Pat had a good friend in Frank, and they soon made contact with their old shooting companion Jeffrey, the solicitor, who had spent all his spare time on the houseboat. Jeffrey had also volunteered and was waiting to join another regiment, but for a few days the three of them were able to meet now and then, have a drink together, and chat about all the old days on the marshes. It helped to pass the time, but they had come there to be soldiers, and everybody wanted to get on with it.

The day came when Pat and Frank and the others in their company were all issued with their new khaki uniforms, and they marched off, as smartly as they could manage, to a proper army camp near Romford. This was where the real military life was to begin, and they were soon doing serious training and endless route marches to toughen them up. They found themselves detailed off to crowded wooden huts, with a bed made of a wooden frame and a piece of canvas nailed across. It was less comfortable, and even more crowded, than the houseboat had been, but they made the best of it. One night Pat and Frank thought they would go off to Southend on the train for a bit of fun, but they managed to get off at the wrong station on the way back, and found themselves spending the night doing yet another route march.

They were moved to another training camp in Sherwood Forest, where they thought they might manage to continue their shooting careers by potting rabbits with catapults, but with singular lack of success. In fact on one illegal expedition to get a rabbit for some of the boys in their hut - everybody was already heartily sick of army stew - they were so embarrassed by their lack of success as hunters that they had to spend their last few shillings in buying a chicken at a farmhouse.

Their next camp, and as it turned out their last in England, was on Salisbury Plain. Training went on as before, amid rumours that they would go abroad next. Someone claimed to have seen uniforms with pith helmets arriving, and it was all round the camp that they were off to East Africa. Then it was announced that foreign service leave would be granted soon. There was still no official destination, but groups of men were sent on leave while the training continued, and it was soon the turn of Pat and Frank.

They were able to spend a few days at the old houseboat, and wandering round the saltings on what they knew must be their last visit to Wells before being pitched into the war in earnest. But it was a bitter-sweet time, for their return home coincided with the arrival of the awful news that Young Ben had already been swallowed up by the war. His ship, the cruiser H.M.S. *Hogue,* had gone down in the North Sea, and he had gone with her. People would soon enough get used to this sort of news, but the abrupt ending of a friend's life so soon after the start of the war seemed unbelievable. The great adventure had a dark side that a young man had hardly thought about until then. You might talk casually of fighting and casualties, but Ben dead already? There was something difficult to grasp in the very idea.

Back at the camp on Salisbury Plain there was still no news of where they would go, but their old training rifles and equipment were replaced by new ones. Next, all weekend passes were cancelled, and they were told to parade in full marching order.

They were off to Southampton, and at last it became apparent what the destination was to be. Their next landfall would be France.

The Battalion was embarked and crossed the Channel one dank, cold, November night. Attack by German submarines was feared, and they were escorted by destroyers that constantly lit up the dark sea with searchlights. Pat and Frank spent the crossing sitting by the funnel of their troop ship, chatting and comparing this night with the many they had spent with their guns on the Wells marshes. Different guns, very different surroundings.

By the cold light of early morning they were landed, and marched off to yet another camp, on French soil this time; then another short march to railway sidings, where they were to board a troop train. There they were wryly amused to see a ramshackle-looking French train made up of cattle wagons, each with its capacity for horses or men painted in large white figures on the side. Someone had obviously worked this out carefully, as they soon found themselves counted aboard, and discovered that they had just enough room to stand inside their wagon, in their full marching order. After much delay the train suddenly jerked into life, so that most of them toppled over, and then struggled to their feet again, already learning to curse French railways and their drivers. This happened regularly as the train made its very slow and jerky progress northwards.

After a while, men got used to this new experience, and each time the train clanked to a halt some would get out and stretch their limbs. As time went on the train went slower and stopped more frequently, for longer periods, until some of the men were finding time to get out, build a fire beside the track, brew up tea in a mess tin, and get back in when the train resumed its asthmatic and uncertain journey. By the end of the day they had arrived at a railhead somewhere behind the Ypres battle front, and everyone thought they were about to have their first taste of the real war. But then orders were received that they were to go to the La Bassée front, some miles to the south, so that instead of marching up to Ypres they marched back towards Bethune.

The next day their company marched out towards where the second battle of Ypres had been raging earlier in the year, and were billeted in some farm buildings in a village that had been heavily shelled; that night they slept in straw with their boots on - the first time they'd had that experience. Their job here, until they were needed to relieve troops holding the line, would be to repair the support trenches behind the line, which had been severely damaged by enemy fire. For the few days they remained here their job consisted of marching up the main La Bassée road every morning to a place that had acquired the nickname of Harley Street, and there repairing the trenches. This was simple, if hard, work; but the approach to it was rendered highly dangerous by the presence of an enemy observation balloon a few miles away.

The German artillery observer in this balloon had a clear view down the La Bassée road, and took a simple delight in calling down fire whenever he saw any movement. Perhaps it is indicative of the inflexible attitude of those running the British army at the time that the company was still expected to march in soldierly manner down the road, in spite of the obvious fact that the sight of them was going to bring down artillery fire every time they did it. The only concession the authorities made was to give orders that the troops should march along the road in small parties, and, if they were shelled, lie down. This was called 'taking cover', but as the whole area had been shelled flat, lying down and hoping that the shrapnel would pass overhead was all you could do.

At night they were still relatively safe and untroubled in their ruined farm buildings, and Pat and Frank were still able to meet and chat about old times. But the day soon came when their company was ordered up to the front to relieve troops in the trenches, and they went in their different directions. Pat had become acting corporal by then, and had duties to attend to in his own section, and when Frank marched off to the front line they could only exchange grins.

Pat's section set out soon after, and they marched up the La Bassée road yet again, for once not worried by the German in the balloon because it was a dull and misty morning with visibility down to a couple of hundred yards. Beyond the place where they had been repairing old shell damage, they came to the beginning of the communication trenches that would take them up to the firing line, and there they had to stand to one side while men coming back for a rest filed past.

The entry to the main communication trench was concealed at the base of a wall, which made it narrow and difficult to get through. As they still waited for their turn to pass through it and approach the front line, the troops leaving the trenches finished trudging back past them, and were followed by stretcher-bearers carrying two wounded men. One of the stretchers somehow got stuck in the narrow entrance to the trench, and the horrified new men found themselves gazing, for what seemed an age, at the soldier who lay in the stretcher. He lay there motionless, apparently gazing at the dull, grey sky, his face and chest gashed by shrapnel and soaked in scarlet blood. He, and the stretcher, and the two men trying to wrestle him through the narrow gap, were all caked with mud. No one made a sound apart from the panting of the struggling stretcher-bearers. Pat and the others stood there, not knowing what to do to help; then with a heave and a muttered curse the stretcher was forced through and it went on its way after the retiring troops. At a brief word from the officer in charge, the new men jumped down into the trench, and began the final two or three hundred yards up to the forward trenches.

They had been prepared for mud, but this trench soon became less like a road or path, and more like the muddy creeks back home on the Norfolk marshes. The whole area had been fought over, and trenches that had once been carefully dug were now badly broken down; earth that had originally been heaped up as a parapet along the top had been washed down into the bottom, so that a foot or two of soft mud was all that the men had to walk or stand in.

When the men of Pat's section reached the position they were to take over, they had to stop and wait for dusk to conceal their movements; they were so close to the German lines that any activity in daylight would soon be detected, and would immediately bring down a rain of fire on their trenches. While they waited they took cover behind one of the great mounds of smashed bricks that were strewn all over this area, which had been a brick works before war had turned it into a wilderness of mud and ruins. Then, when the light faded and they were able to change places with the front line men, came the worst moment. As they watched them struggle back towards them, these men they were to replace were often so deep in mud that they had to stop every few steps to rest, before they could struggle on and fight their way through the quagmire. This, then, was the world they were going to live and fight in, a hole full of mud.

In the front line, as they took their places there, they found that none of the careful trench design they had been learning about seemed to apply any more. Instead of the precise arrangements of trench and dugout shelters they had learned to construct, there were crumbling trenches that were little more than irregular depressions in the ground, and no proper dugouts at all. Here and there, places had been dug in the wall of the trench and roofed with a soldier's groundsheet held up by odd pieces of wood; that was the only shelter from rain or bullet or shrapnel.

Mud was everywhere, so that men had to stand in it all the time, in ordinary parade ground boots and puttees; they still had only the uniforms and gear with which they had left England. In those first days in the line Pat often thought ruefully how much he would have given for the good thigh-length boots he had left behind at home.

In November 1915, the weather seemed to have been wet for ever, and was now very cold. Men were permanently soaked and chilled to the bone, but somehow survived the experience. They slept how they could, huddled under one of the groundsheet shelters, or just leaning against the muddy wall of the trench. Pat felt he had the worst job because, as corporal, he had to see that everyone took their turn on duty, watching over the narrow strip of mud and brick rubble and barbed wire between their trench and the German one, a hundred yards away. Although, as far as they knew, no particular battle was going on, the bombardment from the enemy line continued all the time. Heavy and light artillery, mortars, and the light shrapnel bombs called whizz-bangs all fell steadily on the sodden British line. The Germans seemed to have an infinite supply of weaponry, while the British heavy guns fired so infrequently that it was rumoured that they were only allowed to fire three shells a day each.

Pat and Frank somehow managed to continue to see each other occasionally, and Pat was often surprised at the resilience of the older man, who not only kept up with the rest of his platoon, but managed still to see the funny side of things. At one meeting between them, he told how he had been on the firing step in his trench one night on sentry duty when he saw a German raiding party coming towards them over no-man's land. He watched two figures picking their way towards him in the misty gloom; he had his rifle at the ready and was about to give the alarm and fire when a rocket went up from another position, and revealed two completely immobile posts amongst the old barbed wire and rubble. In the circumstances it was a fairly mild aberration.

At last their company fell back to support positions, where they could get some proper sleep in proper dugouts; but the heavy bombardment went on, and Frank, though as glad as anybody of the chance of lying down in dry blankets, refused to go under-ground, as he said, like a rabbit. He preferred to lie on the ground with his waterproof sheet over him rather than risk being entombed by one of the Kaiser's shells. After they had been a few days in that position, fresh troops came up to take their place, and they were marched back several miles behind the battle for a rest period.

Little real rest was involved, as they had a lot of cleaning up of equipment, and of themselves, to do. There were parades and lectures too, but they had time off, and managed on one occasion to try fishing in a nearby stream. Best of all, there was a village within walking distance where it was still possible to buy something to vary the army rations, and even a glass of wine. They bought some French cigarettes too, but Pat didn't think much of them. Then it was back to the front line again, this time near Givenchy.

Frank amazed Pat again here by volunteering to join a squad that was to raid an enemy trench, and capture and bring back a German for interrogation. Pat tried to dissuade him from joining such an expedition with men half his age, but Frank as usual was sure he could crawl and run and jump in and out of trenches as well as anybody else. Sure enough, a few days later they met again, and he heard the story of the raid, which had been as successful as Frank had said it would be.

He said the worst part was crawling through mud and barbed wire, but the jumping in and out of the enemy trenches had been a breeze. The Germans had beat a hasty retreat down their communication trench as soon as the raiding party had appeared, and their only problem had been that the hand-grenades they were provided with seemed inadequate for the job of blocking off pursuit as they beat it back home again with their prisoner. One of their men had been wounded, but they had got him back to their own trenches, running and dodging as the land between the lines was illuminated by German flares. Frank seemed to have enjoyed it. The thing that had really impressed the raiding party, and their main subject of conversation for a long time, was the great difference in quality between the British and German trenches. The conditions the enemy was living in were luxury, compared to the terrible squalor of their own lines. Instead of inadequate shelter from the elements, let alone gunfire, and deep mud underfoot, the German infantry had well-built trenches and deep, safe dugouts.

Pat often thought about their exploit and the inadequate hand-grenades, and how these dugouts could best be attacked; then a sequence of events occurred which unexpectedly put him in a position where he found that he could do something about it.

It was early in 1916, and the Battalion of which their company was a part was again having a rest period behind the lines. They were packing their kit ready to return to the trenches when the Orderly Sergeant walked up to Pat and handed him an order signed by the Commanding Officer. 'Somebody up there loves you, Corporal,' he said. 'You're not going back to the front. Not today, anyhow.'

The order merely informed Pat that he was to report to the H.Q. of a company of the Royal Engineers at Bethune. Nothing more, not even any instructions about how he was supposed to get there. But orders, especially on a battle front, are orders, and Pat finished packing his kit, shouldered full marching order, and walked the several miles to the town. Here he was interviewed by an Engineer Officer, and asked what his civilian occupation had been, and if he knew anything about explosives. Wondering what information about him had somehow filtered through to the Royal Engineers, Pat gave a brief account of his activities, touching on handling gunpowder and loading cartridges, which of course he was completely familiar with, being a gamekeeper's son. The officer nodded, but made no comment, and he was taken by an N.C.O. to a billet for the night, to spend it wondering what was coming next, and what the morning might hold.

What it held was another meeting with a Royal Engineers Captain, who asked a few questions, and then told him without further preamble that some cases of high explosive were due to be delivered to a chalk pit near the main La Bassée road. Men would be sent to build a suitably protected store there, and he, Pat, would be in charge.

Nobody ever explained why he had been chosen for this work, but after arranging the safe storage of the explosives he found himself, with the R.E. Captain, working on ideas for making precisely the sort of high explosive charges for trench warfare that he and Frank had talked about. He heard that his own Commanding Officer had several times asked for his return to the Sportsmen's Battalion, but this was refused, and Pat found himself no longer existing from day to miserable day in a muddy trench, but in effect running a small bomb factory, and living in the luxury of a tin hut in his chalk pit. It was not the safest possible place to be, with the ever-present possibility of a stray shell falling into the explosives store and blowing them all to kingdom come; but until that happened life would at least be more comfortable.

The bombs that Pat and the assistants he soon acquired were making were of two types. There was a sort of heavy-duty hand-grenade, a tube about a foot long filled with explosives, with a handle for ease of carrying, and a much larger type called a Bangalore torpedo, created especially to destroy barbed wire entanglements. Both these weapons were in great demand as the war entered a phase in which raiding between the trenches became a popular tactic, and Pat and his men were kept very busy in their chalk pit.

The Sportsmen's Battalion continued fighting in the same area, and from time to time Frank was able, during his company's rest periods from the front line, to find his way to the hut in the chalk pit and have a cup of tea and a chat. But then for a long period they did not meet, even when the company was resting nearby, and at last a mutual friend arrived one day to tell Pat the news.

Frank was dead, not from enemy bullet or shell, but from what sounded like a heart attack. He and some other men had been walking back to a village at the rear during a rest period, when a runner arrived with a message to return at once. They ran most of the way back to the company position, and as they collected their equipment Frank fell forward, and died without speaking. Pat found out where he was buried and the following day went and looked for the spot, a patch of earth and a small wooden cross on which was written, 'Pte. Frank Southgate, 2nd Sportsmen's Batt.'

That night in his hut, Pat sat for a long time thinking about the old wildfowling times and the houseboat, and of the two companions whom he would never see there again. When, according to routine, the sentry coming off duty reported to him, Pat asked him in and brewed up some tea. It was just to talk to someone. But there was plenty of work to be done, and in the morning Pat got on with it.

The bomb factory in the chalk pit continued turning out their bombs, at an even faster rate as the fighting warmed up during the early summer, and then the Battle of the Somme started. The Battalion was moved to that area, and Pat received instructions to report to Bethune in full marching order to rejoin his old company. He set about clearing up the hut and getting his gear ready as he was bound to do, but the officer who had given him his orders hinted that the O.C. Engineers was doing his best to get the orders changed, to keep him where he was. Nevertheless, in the morning Pat was in Bethune in his full marching kit, when another messenger appeared and told him to report again to the Royal Engineers H.Q. There, to his great relief, he was asked if he would agree to be transferred from his original regiment to the Engineers.

He had little difficulty in agreeing to that, and was promptly ordered back to his hut again, where he was eventually given the rank of acting sergeant in charge of the explosive works, as the chalk pit was to become. The battle of the Somme, which was supposed to force the Germans back, dragged on without any obvious result but heavy casualties, and Pat heard of the death of others from his old company. From his hut, he often saw the results of the use of his bombs, as the front would light up with flares and heavy bombardment from the enemy lines, in reply to a British raiding party with their Bangalore torpedoes and grenades. In January 1917 Pat received his official transfer to the Royal Engineers, promotion to full sergeant, and even a short spell of leave in England. On the strength of his better rate of pay as a sergeant he married the girl he had been courting in a desultory sort of way before he had left for the war, and after a very brief

honeymoon in London he was back in his explosive works. His
new wife, Claire, was busy with the war too.

She had been a seamstress but, like many girls who found a
new career in those strange times, had taken on an entirely new
sort of job in an engineering works. Aircraft were being built for
the war at the Bolton and Paul works in Norwich, and the country
girl had become a skilled technician working on flying machines.
After Pat went back to France, Claire went on with her war-work,
and it was two more years before they could get on with their
married life.

Eventually German bombardment by heavy artillery became
worse in the area where Pat had his bomb factory, and then the
entire headquarters of his engineer company was moved back. It
was looking as if a new German attack was coming, and Pat was
given sealed orders, marked 'Very Secret, not to be opened except
by orders of the officer commanding'. He could see what was
happening on the La Bassée road, and saw a new regiment, who
he heard were Portuguese troops, being moved up to the front. It
looked as if the Germans knew that these were unseasoned men,
and decided to attack. An intense bombardment started, of both
the front line and rear areas, and lasted for two days. Pat's bomb
factory, being near the main road along which reinforcements
must pass, was in the thick of it, and one of the first shells
destroyed the telephone line that was his only link with his
headquarters. He told his men to leave the bomb works and take

cover in a trench nearby, then waited to see what would happen next.

Soon he saw large numbers of men, too far away to the left to be identified, moving rapidly back; and he reckoned that it was probably the Portuguese front collapsing. He decided that, orders or no, this was the moment to open the Very Secret envelope, which turned out to contain detailed instructions of what to do in the event of an enemy advance. The essence of it was that explosives must not be allowed to fall into enemy hands; he should destroy them and retire with his men to the rear.

It was impossible to make out exactly what was happening, especially with the telephone out of order, but it seemed safe to assume that if the Portuguese were retreating, then the Germans were probably advancing, so he and the bomb-making team began emptying all the stored explosives into a water-filled pit. That done, they returned to cover again, and waited. Pat knew that there was a Scottish regiment in the front line directly ahead of their position, and assumed that, whatever others might be doing, they at any rate were not moving back. By this time night was coming on, and firing had died down, so he decided to stay where they were for the night, and move back in the morning if they had no other orders. Then with dawn, to his great relief, his problem was solved by the arrival of an engineer captain with a lorry, into which they all climbed and were soon bumping and jolting briskly away to safety.

Back at headquarters, now well behind the lines, he reported to the C.O. and was congratulated on getting out with no casualties. He also heard that he had been right in his assessment of the position the previous day; there had indeed been a Scottish battalion in front of them, and the Germans had not been able to break through.

After that, Pat's immediate job was to build a new bomb factory well behind the lines, and then get on with being sergeant in charge of the explosive works again. The war ground on into its last year, with the final German offensive in May 1918, and then in July the big allied counter-attack, but Pat no longer felt very close to it. They still saw fresh troops moving forward now and then, and ambulances never stopped bringing wounded men back, but the war seemed much further away, less personal than in the early days when you knew your close friends were in the trenches almost within sight. The urgency of the bomb-making also slackened off, as the nature of the fighting changed, and by degrees Pat's duties changed too. He was promoted to Company Quartermaster-Sergeant in the end, but by then the bomb-making was over and the war had ended with the armistice.

Then it was just waiting for demobilisation, which seemed very slow indeed to a young man who now just wanted to get back to his wife, and to see Wells and his old friends again. It was April 1919 when the army let him go, with the regulation three medals, and a letter of commendation from his C.O. There had been the hint of a decoration after his very successful evacuation of the old bomb pit in the face of the enemy offensive there, but he had let it be known that he would rather have his rank of acting sergeant made up to full sergeant, and get the extra pay. Somehow this had been arranged. He always seems to have had sympathetic officers to deal with, or perhaps he just had the knack of getting on with them.

Back at Wells again, Pat went straight away to see his old friend Charles. He was the only one of the old wildfowling gang still there, and had changed a lot in the few years the war had lasted. He was much older than the boys, of course, and older than Frank too, but now he had become an old man. They talked about Frank, and how he had died in France, and Charles was able to tell Pat about other Wells boys whom they both knew well, and who had not come back after the war. The old days were clearly over, and Pat turned his back on wildfowling and houseboats and saltings, and set about another new career with his young wife.

Thus, a few years after the war ended, he acquired an old watermill on the Norfolk coast, and became a miller. It meant a lot of hard work, and learning yet another set of skills, but that was nothing new to Pat, and he saw an opportunity in milling, mixing and selling feeding meals. With his knowledge of the sort of feeds in demand on the big sporting estates for pheasant-rearing, he gradually built up a good business, and when there were tourists in the summer Claire sold strawberry teas in the mill garden.

But the old wildfowling days were always there in his heart, and he never stopped going back to the marshes. As time went on there were other good friends who were happy enough to go wildfowling with him on a moonlit night, sometimes to the despair of his wife who, like Ben's wife all those years ago, was not too enthusiastic about it.

No matter how many years passed, whenever he found himself out there on marsh or foreshore at night, with the sound of duck or geese in the dark sky above him, memories of those far-off times at the very beginning of the twentieth century came back and hovered, invisible but very close, in the darkness.

Epilogue

Pat had a long and very active life, first as a miller, then a business man with several different shops, and finally as a local expert with the government War Agricultural Committee during and after the second world war. He and his wife Claire produced two children, first a girl and then a boy; and he died in 1975 in a world that had changed out of recognition from the one he had entered in Queen Victoria's reign. But the sand-hills, and the great expanse of salt marshes that stretch along the north Norfolk coast, were still there; well into his eighties he still took his dog for a walk there every day. Towards the end of his life he also took to writing very popular articles about the marshes and wildfowling for the *Shooting Times*.

When war broke out again in 1939 he was too old to be called up for the regular forces, but he soon joined the Home Guard and took part with his usual enthusiasm. He also demonstrated skills learned in the first war by digging a beautifully-designed dugout for his family. Everyone expected instant bombing at the time, and I well remember, with the rest of the family, being made to sleep in this dugout to avoid air attacks; but no bomb ever fell within a mile of it, and soon we all went back to the comfort of our own beds.

In his last few years, in recognition of his great knowledge of the area, he was appointed honorary warden of the Holkham and Wells marshes by the Nature Conservancy Council, a sort of reprise of his very first job as a boy. A memorial seat stands now where he used to walk at the end of his life, and some of the many visitors who pass the spot these days must wonder who he was. This little book gives a brief sketch of his story.

Mike Cringle, December, 2000.